# LOVE LOST

# LOVE LOST

## Living *Beyond* a
## Broken Marriage

### DR. DAVID B. HAWKINS

**Revell**
Grand Rapids, Michigan

© 2005 by David B. Hawkins

Published by Fleming H. Revell
a division of Baker Publishing Group
P.O. Box 6287, Grand Rapids, MI 49516-6287

Second printing, October 2005

Printed in the United States of America

Library of Congress Cataloging-in-Publication Data
Hawkins, David, Dr.
        Love lost : living beyond a broken marriage / David B. Hawkins.
                p.        cm.
        Includes bibliographical references.
        ISBN 0-8007-5926-5 (pbk.)
        1. Marriage—Religious aspects—Christianity. 2. Separation (Law)—Religious aspects—Christianity. 3. Marriage—Psychological aspects. 4. Separation (Psychology)
        I. Title.
        BT706.H39 2005
        248.8′46—dc22                                                    2004020026

While I have used my clinical experiences throughout this book, all names and situations have been changed to provide anonymity.

# CONTENTS

# 1

## LOVE LOST

*The tears streamed down, and I let*
*them flow as freely as they would,*
*making of them a pillow for my heart.*
*On them I rested.*

Saint Augustine

As the sun rose over the forested hills outside her Northwest home, Trish fidgeted with the covers and wondered what to do. She had awakened several times during the night, fretting about the pending talk with her husband. She feared telling Clint what she had come to realize she must say. Slowly, quietly, she pulled back the covers.

She could barely summon the energy to get out of bed. She glanced out the window, wondering how she would be able to complete today's exercise walk with her friends. She could not seem to clear the fog from her mind. Still, she decided that the walk might give her a little more energy to meet the day.

Trish came to her counseling session with me that afternoon drained. She had been crying before her session and cried throughout the entire hour. She ached as she considered how to tell Clint about the decision she had wrestled with for the past six months. Time had become a blur to her, as had the details of her life. All she could think about was how unhappy she was and how badly she wanted the pain to end. She wearied of the knots in her stomach, the restless nights, the meager appetite, the sullen thoughts. But despite her feelings, telling her spouse her decision would be incredibly hurtful.

She'd told me repeatedly that Clint was not a bad person. In fact, since she had let him know about her unhappiness several months ago, he was trying harder than ever to make a good impression. She had told him that she needed more help with the children and that their finances had to be straightened out. She hated living from paycheck to paycheck, but even more than that, she hated his indifference to the worry it caused her when the bills didn't get paid. His recent efforts seemed like too little, too late. Her feelings had not changed. Even ten years of marriage was not enough glue to hold her to him.

When I saw Trish and Clint together the following week, I could tell something ominous was about to take place. Trish had made her intentions clear during her last session: to tell

Clint that she was no longer in love with him. I worried that this would be a challenging session, and I breathed deeply, hoping to find the reserve in me to be fully present for this couple facing the most horrific event in their marriage.

"Trish, would you like to start?"

She nodded her head slowly. She fumbled with a piece of paper as if she were going to read to us. It had been folded several times, and she worked to straighten it out.

Clint was noticeably anxious. He watched as Trish scanned the paper.

"Are you okay?" he asked.

"I need to tell you something."

"Please don't say that you're going to leave me. I've been working so hard on our marriage. Please don't do anything drastic."

Clint lowered his head, clasping his face with both hands. I said, "Clint, let's let Trish say what she needs to say. Please, Trish, continue."

She began reading from the paper.

"Clint, I need a separation. I don't think I love you anymore, and I need some space to figure out how to find myself again. Our marriage has not been good for either of us. We haven't been happy for a long time."

Clint burst into tears.

"How can you say that? Things have been getting better. I've been trying hard. I've been coming to counseling and meeting with the pastor every week. Please reconsider. Give it a little more time."

"This isn't something I decided yesterday. It may seem sudden to you, but I've been thinking about this for a long time. I'm not saying that our marriage is over. I just need some time to think things through. And I need to look at why I don't love you anymore. I'm sorry to hurt you, Clint. Please know that this is not easy for me, either."

I watched, helplessly, wishing more than anything that I could say some magic words to transform their faltering marriage into the vibrant, dynamic partnership that God intended. For the moment that was not possible. For now, both ached with the pain that only one who has been through this kind of experience can understand.

The extent of pain for those who have endured hearing, or having to say, the words "I don't love you anymore" is hard to understand. I can hardly imagine any more excruciating words. Yet I have seen many people successfully recover from that initial suffering, some by moving on with their lives and others by making step-by-step repairs to their relationship. In either case the path is not easy, but hope does lie ahead.

## An Epidemic of Lost Love

Tragically, this experience is replicated almost weekly in my office. Of all the desperate situations I face, lost love is one of the most heartrending. I watched Trish and Clint face the unspeakable: a love lost in the rubble of years of irritation, alienation, bickering, resentment, and neglect. Neither had spent the requisite time counting the cost of their battles. Both assumed that love could withstand such onslaughts. Both assumed that love could continue, however feebly, amidst the harsh, choking words and insensitivity. They did not think their failure to foster love—a form of benign neglect—could cost so much. No one was there to say, "Stop this before you kill your love for one another. Your hearts can't take the battering."

And so in thousands of homes, in thousands of relationships, love dies or is buried in the ruins of words both spoken and unspoken. It is an epidemic.

You may be reading this book because you too have fallen victim to lost love. You too may have spoken or been told those most painful words, "I don't love you anymore," and felt their toll on your life.

While we hope for the best with these kinds of marital problems, not all marriages survive. Perhaps nothing is as painful and devastating as looking into the eyes of your partner as you are told that the affection you once shared has diminished or died. No one who endures the experience walks away without scars. It would be shallow and ridiculous to offer platitudes in the face of such tumult. No simple offer of consolation does justice to that level of loss. That would be a slap in the face to the magnitude and depth of love lost.

As a small consolation, you should know that others have walked this path and survived. You join many others who have wrestled with rejection and come away stronger than ever. You and your partner can, with diligence, focus on the problems, find solutions, and create a new life—perhaps together, possibly not.

### Christie's Story of Separation

Night comes early in winter in the Pacific Northwest, where I live. We go to work in darkness and return home in darkness. Add a dose of dispiriting dampness and it is easy to become discouraged.

This evening was typical of winter—cold and damp with clouds hung so low you could feel their weight. A drizzle that chilled the bones added to my client's sinking spirits.

Christie sat across from me with a drawn look on her face. The dark circles under her eyes gave evidence of sleepless nights and unresolved grief. Christie held her face in her hands as she spoke that bitter, icy word: *separation.* That single word had torn the fabric of her soul.

She told her story in a rambling manner; I let her talk. I tried to comfort her with my attention, empathy, and a box of tissue.

"I stood at the bottom of the stairs of our apartment, thinking that it couldn't be real. I was being asked to leave the home my husband and I share. I'm not exactly sure when things started to change. In the beginning it was little things that didn't seem to make a difference—we talked less, touched less. But I guess even I can't ignore the fact that the downward spiral has been increasing. What I can't understand is why fifteen years of marriage wasn't enough to keep us from spinning out of control. How could he say that he doesn't love me anymore? I just don't understand that."

Christie paused and looked up at me. She seemed to be reliving the torturous scene as she twisted the moist, fraying tissue in her hands.

"When I looked up at my husband, it was like the ten steps between us were more like ten miles. I felt so small and powerless. I asked him again if it really had to be this way.

I thought we could discuss our problems, perhaps from a new angle. There had to be a way to work things out.

"He said his mind was made up. I don't understand how he could be so strong and hard while I felt so weak and helpless."

Tears streamed down her face. What little strength she retained appeared to be draining away. Even as a professional psychologist, I never get used to the anguish I witness when couples confront the reality that a relationship is broken. I did my best to reassure her.

"I don't think I would say you were being weak. Most people would feel devastated if their spouse asked them to leave their home and marriage. Everyone I know who has heard those words and faced a separation has been overwhelmed. You are entitled to feel bad. You are also entitled to grieve. This is a huge loss."

My words didn't seem to reach her. She continued to cry. Her face was streaked with tears, her mascara stained her cheeks, her eyes were red and puffy.

"I know our marriage wasn't perfect. In fact, I can't say that I never thought of leaving. My husband and I have been through some tough times, but whenever we reached a crisis we decided to stick with it. During those times, we always agreed that marriage is a sacred, unbreakable trust. Somehow we would make things work out. To be told to leave is so horrible. I can't seem to make sense of it no matter how hard I try."

"Did you see it coming?" I gently asked.

She slouched further into the overstuffed chair, glancing at the watercolor on my wall as though she was hoping to find some answers there.

"Yes and no," she replied. "I suppose the distance between us began years ago and I just didn't want to see it. This past year certainly has been challenging for us. Maybe that's why he needed his space."

"And what happened this past year?"

Christie went on to share a story I have heard hundreds of times over the past twenty years. It's the story of broken promises, broken lives, and lost love. These are the ingredients for trouble, and they often lead to separation and many times divorce. Sometimes these separations produce healthier, stronger marriages as couples work at understanding their conflicts and seek to remedy them. But many times the separation is simply the beginning of the end. Regardless of the end result, understanding how to make sense of rejection is necessary to bring personal healing and deeper faith.

## Death of a Dream

Nothing is quite as chilling as the cold splash of "I don't love you anymore." Most people should, but often don't, see it coming. When they step back and examine the facts unflinchingly, they can sometimes identify the warning signs that led up to the final words. But few are willing to critically look at the harsh reality that signals the end of the dream. Most of us prefer to keep doing what we've been doing for years, comfortable in the rut we have carved out.

We clench our fists around what we claim as "mine!" We desperately want to hold on, although only a shell of a marriage remains. We resist change of any kind, clinging to the fantasy of what we thought the marriage could be or hoped it would be in the future. We refuse to see what the relationship has become. And if we do that for too long, solving the problems becomes impossible.

Many truths require time for gestation. They cannot be rushed and, ironically, often need the temporary cocoon of denial in order to grow into solid pieces of wisdom that can stand on their own. Denial is needed for a time if your partner has announced the end of your relationship. Denial offers us time and space to deal with the immensity of a situation one piece at a time. He or she did not come to that conclusion quickly, in spite of what you might believe. Likewise, time is needed to break through the many masks of denial to fully appreciate the fact that the dream has faded and that changes must occur. You certainly need to take some time before telling a partner that you have not been happy in the relationship for a long time and now want out.

As you go through the painful process of re-membering (re-attaching), gathering into yourself those parts of your relationship that you have tried to leave behind and reflecting on how you came to be where you are, be gentle with yourself. Be kind toward all that is unfinished in your heart. Honor the wisdom that has come from the place that you have traveled. One day you will know why life's events have occurred as they have.

There are no wasted steps in God's economy. One day as you look back you will say "yes" to all that has happened, no matter how difficult. You will recognize that all of your experiences have been a necessary part of the learning process, leading you to a fuller and richer life. For now you

know in part, but one day you will understand it all (see
1 Cor. 13:9).

## Letting Go, Holding On

So much of life seems to be about letting go and holding
on or, as the Scriptures aptly describe the change process,
letting a seed fall to the ground to die, then waiting patiently
for spring when the sprouts of new life burst forth. This
will, by necessity, be a time of letting go of old patterns of
relating. Old patterns must be relinquished to give space
to new ways of communicating and understanding. You
will need time to digest all that has happened, why it has
happened, and what can be done about it. Quick, frantic
actions will not be effective.

Impatience, intolerance, and harshness are perhaps the
greatest enemies of the deep, personal work required during this time. Impatience and a strong desire to keep doing
things the way we have always done them will hinder progress. Who wants to admit personal failure or weakness?
But a tragedy of this magnitude requires the patience and
courage to let things fall apart, because that must be done
before new growth can take place.

Gentleness is the antidote to harshness. During this excruciating and volatile time, gentleness toward yourself and
your spouse will be a wonderful salve. This will not be an
easy time for either partner. Whether you are leaving or
being left, it will be gut-wrenching and require both of you
to dig deep into yourselves to find the kindest person you
can be.

Perhaps the Scripture most fitting for this or any strained encounter is the advice of the apostle Paul: "Do not let any unwholesome talk come out of your mouths, but only what is helpful for building others up according to their needs, that it may benefit those who listen" (Eph. 4:29).

What exactly does your partner need? Can you give it as a supreme act of love?

**Roller Coaster Emotions**

Not all broken relationships are alike. However, love lost often leads to a separation at some point. For some the separation is a death knell, the ending of a long and painful process. In these cases the death of the marriage has already occurred, so separation can be experienced as freedom. Perhaps much of the anguish has been worked through, little by little, over a long period of time. The separation may be a final acknowledgment that the marriage has truly ended. Finally, you feel relief. Even in these situations, however, new layers of grief will be discovered.

> *Sometimes all we can do when the challenge comes and we feel our parts flying to their edges is hold on and wait.*
>
> Gloria Karpinski

But for Christie, like so many others, the separation was not welcomed and came like a sucker punch to the gut. She had felt relatively content in her marriage. She watched as her husband languished in his confusion. Unable to rescue him, she waited for the crisis to pass so that they could resume their comfortable, middle-class lifestyle. She assumed that he would eventually resolve his seemingly unfounded bitterness and wake up to their good life. But while she was waiting came the words that caused irreparable damage: "I don't know how I feel about you anymore. I want to live on my own. I'm not sure I even love you."

> *Be still, and know that I am God.*
>
> Psalm 46:10

There they were, the words she had hoped he would not utter. Short of breath and feeling dazed, she was still supposed to go to work and carry on as if nothing were happening. But her world as she knew it was unraveling.

The days and weeks following her husband's announcement took Christie on the emotional roller coaster ride of her life. In the midst of intense, shifting emotions, she struggled to maintain focus at work. One moment she felt there was little worth living for; the next she felt a glimmer of hope that reconciliation could occur.

Nothing helped. She tried to will herself to feel better and think positively. She knew there was always hope—God can do the impossible—so she clung to that hope like a castaway anchors himself tenaciously to a makeshift raft on the high seas.

Work was both a blessing and a curse. The first several weeks were incredibly challenging. She was a computer programmer for a government agency, so her responsibilities required keen attention to detail. This was hard for her to muster as she languished in the depths of despair. Yet at times she was grateful for her work. It provided a temporary respite from the storm, a time when she did not have to sit home wondering what her husband was thinking and doing. Obsessing about him and their former life together did nothing to improve her emotional life. Work was a familiar world, one where she had a shred of control.

She was forced to her knees, as are most of us when faced with heartbreaking circumstances. While she was tempted to panic and react haphazardly, wise counsel told her to sit tight and find the center of the storm. Prayer brought her a desperately needed measure of peace, although she sometimes gave in to the temptation to react out of hurt and fear and speak biting words to her husband in an attempt to give back a bit of the pain she was experiencing.

## A Time to Wait

Couples often separate because one partner has asked for the dreaded "space" that seems impossible to give. This is a time when the jilted person wants to demonstrate a capacity to love, learn, and listen. Waiting does not come easily for the lost and bereft.

Indeed, many learn something new out of this tragedy: the art of planting seeds and waiting for them to germinate. We have been told that good things take time, but patience is a hard premise to practice. To lose love is to lose a most vital part of life. We often panic. Fear and desperation creep into the secret places of the heart. In our hurry to rebuild the relationship, we often make a mess of things. Most who have been involved in a marital separation know about the ill-timed comment and the rushed phone call begging the lover to return home. These abrupt moves rarely meet our desired ends. Instead they sink us deeper into the quagmire that got us to this point in the first place.

A favorite writer of mine, Sue Monk Kidd, writes in her wonderful book *When the Heart Waits* about the transformation of the caterpillar.[1] She eloquently unravels the mystery of the chrysalis and the development of caterpillar to butterfly. The parallels to our lives are unmistakable. Staring at a tiny bundle of threads hanging in a tree, you would be convinced that life is absent. Nothing moves. No activity suggests that change is occurring. The months crawl by, but watching the cocoon and willing things to change is a useless act. After the long winter, the first hint of movement is seen. Life has indeed been developing in that resting place, and what emerges is miraculous. Likewise, left alone to do what must be done, without unnecessary tampering, we can become free. This is the only way to become the winged monarch.

The lesson is clear: Many times the best thing to do in a crisis is nothing. Nothing active, that is. Waiting is often the best plan of all.

Although waiting goes against our natural instincts to scurry about and try to fix everything immediately, we need to allow ourselves time to be still to collect our thoughts. Look to the Lord and in the quiet hear the loving voice that soothes and comforts.

### Is This Human Nature?

Christie's story is not unique. The statistics are so overwhelming yet so familiar that we are numb to them. We may be surprised when another couple separates, but it will be old news in a few weeks. Marriages are just as likely to dissolve as they are to succeed, whether the couple is in the church or out. Christian or non-Christian, whatever belief system you subscribe to or philosophy you endorse—marriage is a perilous journey.

Should we be so surprised by the rate at which marriages and other relationships disintegrate? While this is both sad and tragic, perhaps it is not terribly surprising when we think about human nature.

First, *humans have been estranged from one another since the beginning of time.* Ever since the Garden of Eden, we have pointed fingers of blame at one another. Eve blamed the serpent, while Adam blamed Eve and God. They both refused to own up to their part in the problem. Neither stepped up to say, "I'm sorry. I was wrong." Time has changed nothing. We are just like them. What kind of relationships can be developed under those conditions?

A scrutiny of the early biblical account shows the rift in relationships developing from the onset. While we hope for the best, deep down we seem to know that we are swimming upstream. We know the depravity that exists in our hearts and wonder if we can really sustain love for anyone other than ourselves.

Second, *pride enters the scene and creates further dissension.* Most of us would rather walk on hot coals than admit we were wrong. We want to protect our flagging self-esteem and are willing to blame our spouse, no matter the cost to the marriage. We know intellectually that this will only ruin our most prized possession, yet we seem unable to stop the free fall.

Pride, of course, was alive and well in the Garden of Eden and lives within each of us. We want to protect ourselves and are willing to sling arrows at others to ensure that we are right. Not surprisingly, this strategy does not work. Our foibles and failures are ultimately revealed, but usually after the damage has already been done.

Third, *human nature seems fraught with a pervasive sense of childish entitlement and selfishness.* We not only want to blame others but also want our own way. Moreover, we feel entitled to it. We want to maintain rigid control of our world. The two-year-old is alive and well in most of our marriages. We have not learned the elementary school principles of sharing and helping one another. We want what we want when we want it. Unfortunately, this quality kills and destroys our marriages.

Finally, *because many are stuck in their immaturity, they are unable to be sacrificial in their loving.* Mature love, as the Scriptures describe it, is required in order for love to blossom. However, mature love requires that we set aside our own agendas and acknowledge that the needs of others are more important than our own (see Rom. 12:3). This sacrificial quality is hard to find in relationships today, partially explaining the high rate of separation in marriages.

Rainier Maria Rilke, the famed German poet, writes often about love and its difficulties.

> To love is good, too: love being difficult. For one human being to love another: that is perhaps the most difficult of all our tasks, the ultimate, the last test and proof, the work for which all other work is but preparation.[2]

Rilke and others like him aren't exactly optimistic when it comes to marriage. M. Scott Peck, in his overwhelmingly popular book *The Road Less Traveled*, also challenges us to see life as difficult. He focuses on revealing our narcissistic nature and gives a clarion cry that love can succeed only after we reach the end of our childish yearnings.[3]

## Anatomy of a Separation

What exactly happens when love unravels? Why is it so devastatingly painful? Why do many even consider ending their lives when faced with the challenge of a decomposing relationship?

Perhaps that is it: Life as we know it is decomposing. Something has died. Even if the marriage survives, the separation slaps us in the face with the fragile reality of love and marriage. The marriage that we invested ourselves in so fully is frighteningly vulnerable.

What is it like to be so vulnerable? Tamara knows only too well.

## Tamara's Story

"He can't seem to decide whether he wants to be married to me or run around and act like a teenager," Tamara said angrily. "He wants to have his cake and eat it too. He complains that our marriage is stale and leaves me for another woman. I died a thousand times because of what he did to me. But even worse than that, he won't leave me alone. He wants to come over to see the kids and me all the time. It drives me crazy.

"It was terribly hard to take at first. He left me for another woman and said that he didn't love me anymore. I assumed it was because I was too heavy, not sexy enough, and didn't make enough money. He said he was just tired of our relationship, but I still wonder what the real issues are. I could think of a thousand things wrong with me, all the stuff that I've struggled with my whole life. Jeff leaving me just brought all the skeletons out of my closet. Now I'm trying to figure out who I am and what to do with a husband who loves me but isn't 'in love with me.'"

Tamara continued, sharing the hurt suffered during the separation and betrayal. While she appeared angry, it was clear that there was a great deal of pain just below the surface.

"I hate those words, *not in love with me*. He still loves me enough to come see me and the kids, but not enough to be committed to us. I can't trust him anymore."

Tamara is frightened about her future. She feels unsure of her self-worth. Jeff says he wants to pay support so that his children are well cared for and so that their lifestyle does not change, but Tamara is not sure it will last. Her trust has been broken. She has been betrayed and feels incredibly vulnerable. She has experienced a loss of innocence that may never be recaptured.

Because of her new distrust, she wonders what will change next. Jeff has proven to be unstable and unpredictable, so she knows she will need to learn to rely on herself. To protect herself she has begun to squirrel away money for potential problems in the future.

Lost love and the separation that often ensues lead to a cascade of challenges. Tamara's lifestyle has changed. While Jeff is being helpful now, she knows that they cannot continue to live this way. They are in a "holding pattern." He remains involved with his family while continuing to see another woman. Tamara has yet to force him to make a decision. She knows that once she does, his behavior may become even more unpredictable.

**The Dangling Separation**

Tamara's story represents one of the myriad ways couples separate. It is a far too common picture of a relationship unraveling thread by thread. In Tamara's case, her husband went in search of a younger, shinier version of the woman he had loved for many years. He mistakenly believed that he could hold onto the wonderful qualities that he admired in his wife while replacing some of the troublesome traits with a new, improved model.

Understandably, Tamara struggles with this situation. While her friends clamor for her to stop allowing her husband to come over, she holds onto the slightest signs of hope and avoids rejecting him for fear that he will not contact her at all. What she cannot see is that Jeff needs to experience his own dose of reality: that he *cannot* have his cake and eat it too. He will have to make a choice.

The dangling separation is perhaps the worst kind for a marriage. It can actually be described as a non-separation separation, because one partner wants to pretend that it is not really happening. Thus, all the damaging aspects of the troubled marriage are perpetuated with none of the potentially helpful aspects of a separation occurring. In situations like this, one partner must strike up enough courage to make a clean break so that the healing process can begin.

## A Lost Covenant of Love

Whether a marriage fractures with one quick snap or dies a slow death, a powerful bond is broken. Certainly God knew of the agony that would result if the indivisible were divided. From the book of Genesis we learn that God destined man and woman to be united to complement one another and that the cleaving of one to the other would fashion a bond like no other. From the beginning, man and woman were created to live inseparably in harmony.

But God also knew that sin would enter into the world and with it would come a veritable landslide of calamities. He knew that relationships would suffer from violence, unfaithfulness, and betrayal, and that separation and divorce would result. So while marriage is an inseparable knitting of souls, it is also an easily torn tapestry of spirit because of the sin which taints all relationships.

The heart of Scripture is about reconciliation; however, men and women are given free will to choose their paths, often leading to painful consequences. Scripture tells us that marriage is not something to be treated lightly. Rather, marriage has been designed as a covenant between man and wife, similar to God's covenant with his people (Gen. 2:24; Matt. 19:4–6). God designed marriage to be a sacred institution. It is not simply a civil ceremony between two parties. It is a tripartite union of man, woman, and God. God is a witness to the vows that we have taken and is also part of that union. When love is lost and separation occurs, a sacred trust is violated.

## Summary

Any heartfelt union of love is an intricate weaving of separate spirits. When that love is lost, one must expect severe repercussions, most often unremitting pain and grief. Many couples will work diligently to discover together a new love that they had not known before. However, others will struggle constantly to overcome the obstacles and piece together again a less than satisfactory relationship that has suffered extensive damage. One cannot help but wonder if this kind of marriage should be "saved." Many couples, sadly, end up bouncing back and forth in separation after separation until, exhausted, one person finally files the legal papers. Regardless of the final outcome, every life of lost love contains deep sadness and grief, which will be the topic of our next chapter.

# 2

## THE MYSTERIOUS GRIEF OF LOVE LOST

*In the depth of winter, I finally learned
that within me there lay an invincible
summer.*

Albert Camus

Few words are harsher than "I don't love you anymore." These are deadly words, capable of piercing even the most callous heart. We all want to love and be loved. Only those hurt and hardened will stand stoically in the shadow of lost love.

For the rest of us—those who care deeply, feel deeply, and are still willing to be touched by another's love—hearing someone say "I don't love you anymore" can send us into a dark place. Those speaking these words of sorrow and separation may be equally devastated. Regardless of the circumstance, these are never easy words to hear or say. *Never.*

Some people attempt to soften the blow by rallying to see every loss as an opportunity for growth. They offer platitudes and clichés as a ray of hope for the future. We can find opportunity in every adversity that we face, they say.

They are right that if we had no hope we could scarcely push on. But a serious darkness must be considered first. Before we reach the light, we must face a brutal truth: We experience an immeasurable and unavoidable loss when we traverse the territory of lost love. There is simply no way around it, no way to sugarcoat it. It is not pretty, and it is not pleasant. One must summon incredible courage to face the realization that things will never be the same. If you are able to move forward to a place of healing, you will accomplish it one step at a time, not in a single sprint.

I admit that not all who experience lost love are paralyzed by dread. Some have weighed out the alternatives and decided that it was best to end the relationship. But many have had this path chosen for them or have made the decision with an edgy reluctance. Regardless of how you have entered this place of lost love and possible pending separation, you are experiencing a potent loss.

Judith Viorst, in her book *Necessary Losses*, describes lost love, separation, and possible divorce as being similar in many ways to death. She notes:

> Although my focus here is on mourning the death of those we love, I should mention the other marital death called divorce. For the breakup of a marriage is like the death of a spouse, and will often be mourned in closely parallel ways. There are some important distinctions: Divorce evokes more anger than death, and it is, of course, considerably more optional. But, the sorrow and pining and yearning can be as intense. The denial and despair can be as intense. The guilt and self-reproach can be as intense. And the feeling of abandonment can be even more intense—He didn't have to leave me; he chose to leave me.[1]

Viorst gives a compelling argument for the enormity of lost love, separation, and divorce. These experiences are traumatic, and the feelings can approximate those of an actual death in your life. Let's look more closely at the symptoms of grief that come with lost love as seen through the story of Carl and Sarah.

## Carl and Sarah

It was a stifling hot summer morning. Sarah heard the garage door rattle open as Carl left for the electrical supply store where he worked as manager. Sarah would need to rise soon to ready the kids for school before leaving for the bank where she worked as a lead teller.

Lying in the stillness, she wondered if he would come home for dinner or stay out late with the guys again. In recent months, a troubling pattern had developed which threatened their marriage. Tension had been growing as Sarah became more and more frightened about Carl's distance and time spent away from the family.

She had talked to Carl many times about her feelings, but her concerns were met with defensiveness and accusations that she was being controlling. Every argument she gave for him to stay home with her and their children brought a new escalation of the conflict. Given this antagonistic environment, she feared unfaithfulness on his part, though he vehemently denied any wrongdoing. She noticed chilling bits of evidence to the contrary, however: unusually late nights, money missing from their checking account, phone calls taken in private.

The incessant arguing began taking its toll on their relationship. Family time and tenderness both disappeared. Resentment became the mortar in the brick wall between them.

Sarah grew weary of their bitter exchanges. The sleepless nights drained her energy, and the hostility between them eroded the love she once had for him. After months without any promise of relief, she began making plans for a separation. Twice before she had threatened the action without serious intention, but now she considered what a separation might actually entail. Where could she and the children actually go? How would she support them? Would Carl help her, or would he threaten to withhold money and support, forcing her to rely on her limited earnings and assistance from her parents that she dreaded to ask for? But her fears only fueled her anger and determination to make it on her own.

One evening when Carl was again out late with his friends, Sarah decided to make the break. She called her parents and told them the situation. When they arrived, she loaded the children into their van. She scribbled a note to Carl announcing her intent to separate. She told him not to contact her because she needed some time on her own to think things through.

The following days were agonizing for both Carl and Sarah. Though he previously had been insensitive to her feelings, he missed her intensely. He now had time to consider how much he cared about Sarah and their two daughters. He did not want to lose them. His calls to her parents' home were answered by his stern father-in-law. Sometimes Carl could hear Sarah weeping in the background. She longed to talk to him, but she maintained a shaky resolve to keep her distance as she considered her options.

Sarah tried to go back to work after the separation but found it difficult to concentrate; her thoughts focused on Carl and what he might be doing. She missed his ability to make her laugh even in the most serious of situations. She missed his warmth in their bed at night. But she did not miss the fighting. And she could not say for sure that she loved him any longer. Many struggles had chiseled away at those feelings. Although she was distraught, she told herself that she had done the right thing and needed to tend to her children, who needed her now more than ever. While they begged for answers, she offered the little bits of support and consolation she could muster. Waves of grief flooded her as she ached for a return to a normal marriage and family.

Carl, too, struggled. He tried to soothe his pain by spending time with friends. They assured him that Sarah would be back soon. He hoped they were right, but he knew he faced a tremendous challenge. Would he run after her, pacify himself with late nights with his friends, or take time to consider his life and behavior?

Both Sarah and Carl grieved. They had a hard time thinking of anything other than one another. Attempts to be "strong" gave way to tears. Sleep was often fitful, interrupted by panic and fear. "What if?" they wondered. Both began facing the unutterable possibility that their relationship might be over. With that thought came gut-wrenching sobs. Both reminisced about days past when they would have done anything to please the other. Now they found themselves on opposite sides of a great divide.

After they had been separated for several months, Sarah had to stretch to remember any feelings of fondness for Carl. Sitting with her parents in their living room one evening, she said the words aloud for the first time: "I don't think I love him anymore."

## The Many Faces of Grief

Facing the reality of lost love is, for most people, an excruciating crisis. Our worlds are turned upside down. Every aspect of our lives is disrupted. Our stomachs are in knots; sleep is fitful; appetite is absent. All of the usual moorings are gone, for if we cannot count on feeling safe, loved, and in love with our partner, what can we count on? Our constantly muddled thoughts make it feel as though we are slogging through quicksand. We are experiencing grief in its fullest form. This inner aching feels like emotional disintegration. We literally feel as though we are coming apart at the seams.

What should you expect as you face this season of grief? Elisabeth Kübler-Ross, in her groundbreaking book *On Death and Dying,* gave us the words to describe what happens to us when facing severe loss. Although she was speaking of grief after a loved one's death, her message was equally applicable to lost love. She said that grief unfolds in stages: denial, anger, bargaining, depression, and acceptance. The stages may be clear, but they don't often unfold neatly.[2] Let's take a closer look at some of the feelings you may experience while moving through grief over your damaged relationship.

### Disbelief

The first reaction of most people facing the prospect of lost love is denial and disbelief. "How could this have happened to me?" we wonder. "This is not the script I had for my life. Things weren't supposed to turn out this way." After all, most of us believed we entered the relationship "for better or for worse, for richer or for poorer." Who would have imagined the day when we would violate that contract?

This loss of innocence is a profoundly disturbing experience. One moment we are married, standing in front of a mirror preparing ourselves for a new day; the next we are alone in a new apartment, facing an unknown figure in the mirror. As we face the mirror, we see a tear-stained face, a person bedraggled from another sleepless night, hair as unruly as life itself. "Who is this new person?" we ask. "Where did she come from? How in the world did I get from there to here?"

### Numbness

After the initial shock of feeling a knife to the heart, the mind rushes in to protect us from the next blow. Denial often takes on the form of numbness, which sets up an invisible barrier to the daggers of pain thrust at the heart. It tries to keep us from feeling the agony all at once.

This anesthetic has limited ability, however. Numbness will come and go, like the throbbing that comes with a sprained ankle. We may be able to forget about the crisis for a while, but the dull ache comes back, reminding us that all is not well.

Dr. Thomas Whiteman and Randy Petersen discuss this issue of denial and numbness in their book *Starting Over:* "In our experience with divorce recovery, six months is a reasonable period for denial. We're not holding a stopwatch to you, but if it's eight or nine months after the fact and you're still pretending that nothing serious happened, you're probably stuck in the denial stage. . . . The duration will vary, depending on the timing and severity of the shock involved."[3]

### Sadness

The most familiar face of grief is sadness. For many, it comes as a pit-in-the-stomach kind of feeling that is accompanied by tears. We ache and pine with the thought of the lost loved one. Carl tells how he experienced his loss.

"I was the one left, or dumped, as they call it. I didn't want the relationship to end, and I begged her to give me another chance. But she had her mind made up. She said she no longer loved me. I cried and cried until I thought I couldn't cry another tear. I felt sad for hours, looking out the window wondering how I was going to cope. I missed her so much even before she told me it was over. The waves of tears came and went. There were many times when I thought I was moving on, then I felt horrible again."

Carl's experience is not unusual. Many feel lost after their loved one leaves. They know that they must carry on with their daily tasks but find it hard to do so because their grief is overwhelming.

The Scriptures grant us numerous examples of biblical heroes who felt caught in the web of sadness. One of them, King David, had his season of anguish after losing his son to a premature death. "David pleaded with God for the child. He fasted and went into his house and spent the nights lying on the ground. The elders of his household stood beside him to get him up from the ground, but he refused, and he would not eat any food with them" (2 Sam. 12:16–17). Here was a miserable man. Unable to eat, sleep, or participate in any normal activities of daily life, David was enveloped in grief.

But, thankfully, sadness lasts but a season. Three verses later we read that "David got up from the ground. After he had washed, put on lotions and changed his clothes, he went into the house of the LORD and worshiped. Then he went to his own house, and at his request they served him food and he ate" (v. 20).

We can expect that sadness will slowly give way to normal feelings, although when you are in the middle of your struggle it is hard to believe that. But mourning lasts for a season, and joy indeed comes in the morning.

A word of caution: Some may find that they need an extra boost in order to return to a semblance of their former life. This boost may take the form of medications specifically designed for situations like this. A physician may prescribe commonly used antidepressants to give you the lift you need when your systems are overwhelmed.

Separation is enough to overcome the hardiest of people. Sarah usually handled stress with ease. But in this case she could not seem to regain her focus and ability to work. She was encouraged to talk to her physician about possible medications. At first she felt that it was a disgrace to ask for medical help, but she decided it was necessary. She found herself crying more than usual for weeks after the separation, and her sleep and appetite were erratic. She acknowledged that she needed more help to get through this very difficult time. She was reassured by her physician that overwhelming stress can cause a biochemical imbalance in many people. At those times restorative medications are essential.

### Confusion

After three weeks of separation from her husband of fifteen years, Sarah sat across from me with tear-stained cheeks. She cried quietly, unable to articulate her pain.

"It's okay," I said. "You don't have to try to explain your feelings to me. Just be with your pain."

"Good," she said softly, "because I don't think I could tell you what I am feeling. I just feel like a blob of crummy feelings. I just hurt. And I can't think straight."

She continued to analogize her experience. "I feel like I am traveling in a foreign country where I don't speak the language or know the customs. What's worse, I'm not sure where I am. I'm not sure if I am in hostile or friendly territory. Will I be ambushed and hurt in some way? I can't focus on what people are saying. All I know is that they seem to be going on with their business while I struggle to make sense out of my life."

Sarah was experiencing one of the more troubling aspects of grief: confusion. Most of us are geared to want to put things in perspective. We want to be in control, in that place where life is predictable. It is so difficult just to be with our experience without fully understanding it or attempting to exert some control over it.

Kari West and Noelle Quinn, in their book *When He Leaves,* write, "Under normal circumstances a person's energy is distributed equally in four areas: spiritual, physical, mental, and emotional. During divorce, 85 percent of your energy goes to emotional coping. The remaining 15 percent goes to the other areas combined. That's why, running low on spiritual energy, you have trouble praying; low on mental energy, you have trouble concentrating; low on physical energy, you feel exhausted."[4]

### Rejection

Someone you cared about and shared myriad experiences as well as emotional and physical intimacy with has set you aside. Rejection! Whether or not you were the one to initiate the separation, events leading up to the separation also included feelings of rejection and a palpable fear and anger.

Both Carl and Sarah felt rejection. While it was Sarah who initiated the actual separation, she had felt abandoned by Carl for months. Now, during the separation, both nursed grudges at having been left by the other. Their limited conversations were speckled with barbs that betrayed their anger and pain. Both felt the sting of rejection and the fear of permanently losing love.

If you have let the immensity of your current situation sink in, you have felt the consuming anger that accompanies rejection. In the wake of lost love and possible separation, as well as with the fear of divorce, comes the inner rage that masks the wound to your soul. You ask, "Why couldn't he love me for who I am? Why did he have to step outside the sacred bounds of marriage? Why couldn't he love and honor me as he promised?"

Anger leads to resentment, that brooding, visceral feeling of power—a sense of power to do damage to the person who has wronged you. You feel a righteous indignation. They are the villain and you are the victim. Of course, at some level you know it isn't true, but for this season, you indulge yourself in these feelings.

Soon enough, however, you will realize that remaining angry does no one any good. You certainly are not hurting your ex-mate with your fantasies of revenge. You know that you must move forward with your life, and resentment keeps you stuck in a negative attachment to the past. This is not the place you want to live. But how do you move beyond anger? Here are some important steps:

1. Let yourself feel your feelings. Let yourself be good and angry.
2. Find a good friend who will let you embrace your anger without becoming consumed by it.
3. Remember that there is a season for anger, but then it is time to move toward forgiveness.
4. Begin to see your role in the relational problems and the difficulties that led up to them.
5. Accept that you are human, understanding that both of you did the best you could at that particular time in your lives.

Perhaps the most important thing that you can do with your anger is *learn from it*. Anger, while terribly uncomfortable, can be very instructive. It can reveal areas of our lives where we are selfish, demanding, or naïve. During this critically painful time, consider journaling as well as meditating on your pain. Journaling will bring you closer to what is happening within you and help you gain perspective on all that is happening to you.

Prayerfully ask God to heal your deepest wounds as well as reveal your heart's hidden motives. Intense emotions can lead us into deep spiritual healing. These times of raw emotion will help us grow in ways we have never imagined. We can become more compassionate and more spiritual by learning to rely on the Lord in new ways. Our relationships with others will also improve as we mature spiritually.

## Grief Disguised

The human psyche is an ingenious creation. Since the beginning of time we have come up with an incredible array of tools and techniques to soothe our heartache. Unable to deal with the full weight of our loss, we devise strategies, often unconscious and repetitious, to avoid the onslaught of affliction.

### Attempts at Control

When love is slipping away, we have an innate tendency to hold on even tighter to the illusion of the relationship. No one wants to sit back and watch the semblance of love drift farther away. Subsequently, many make the dire mistake of grabbing onto, clutching, and squeezing the lover in the hope that they can retain what is left of their love. But this tactic is destined to fail. Your lover has made a decision, and you cannot make them fall back in love with you. Love and affection cannot be forced; you must settle into a different mode of relating—one that requires patience, trust, and hope.

These vain attempts at control are all forms of disguised grief. They are efforts we make to stall the inevitable. We do not want to have to face grief head on. We desperately want to believe that a valiant effort can save the day. But no, it only muddies the water, adding to the confusion and the overwhelming emotions.

### Busyness

Many disguise their grief with apparent composure. They act as if nothing significant has happened and become even busier than normal. The routines of everyday life keep lovesickness behind a wall of denial. Busyness is greeted as a welcome respite from focusing on the pain.

Garth experienced his loss with typical male stoicism. He was thirty when he decided to end his marriage. He had been unhappy for nearly three years but had stayed with his wife out of obligation and concern for their two children. Eventually, however, his determination wore thin, and he awoke one morning having decided that this was to be the day. He saw no sense in putting it off. He was not doing anyone any favors by staying with the family out of duty. So he made the decision and moved his things out that evening. Initially, he thought he was adjusting fine. He immersed himself in work and received accolades for his efforts. The reality of his immense loss did not surface until months later.

"I guess I was like most men," Garth said. "I made the decision and tried to get on with life. That's what all my friends told me to do—get on with my life. I began seeing other women right away and didn't give myself any time to really think about what was happening to me. I kept myself wrapped up in work, dating, and having fun. Whenever I started to feel the doldrums surface, I just dug in and did something about it. It never occurred to me to slow down and listen to my feelings."

But Garth's anesthetic began to wear off, and he started feeling depressed. Increased work did nothing to ward off "the blues." Sleepless nights and exhaustion made it difficult to concentrate at work. Friends and family noticed that he was less happy. Garth used more of his limited energy to push away the slumbering sadness, but to no avail. One day waves of grief and tears erupted without notice.

### Hypersexuality

Our society has proclaimed from its billboards and television programs that sexuality will cure any malaise. Many people run wildly from grief in search of as much excitement as they can manage. They believe that sex is the answer to the pain.

"Get on with your life." This was the counsel given to Amy when Jack left her unexpectedly. He had found adventure in "greener pastures," so why shouldn't she do the same?

Her friends were well-meaning, but they were also short-sighted and simplistic. After all, who wants to give their friends the following advice? "Amy, what you need to do now is be quiet and sit with your pain. You need to lean into your discomfort, cry your tears, embrace your sadness."

You are not likely to receive that advice. You will probably be told to get out there and fish in the great pond of life for someone to help you forget your sorrow. But make no mistake, this method will not work! It may delay the pain for the moment, but it simply will not work as a long-term solution.

Amy did what many do to comfort her rejected heart: She found another man offering affection and passionate sex. For a while she thought she had discovered the fountain of youth in addition to leaving the well of grief behind. But soon the sexual excitement began to wear off. Let's hear the story from her.

"I am sick about how I handled the separation. I felt terrible when Jack left me. I felt worthless. I was scared to death that no one would find me attractive. Jack told me that he didn't love me anymore, and for years before that he had told me everything that was wrong with me. I guess I was extremely vulnerable to anyone paying the least attention to me.

"Well, I started accepting invitations by some women at work to go out and have a few drinks. I didn't think that would hurt anything, but before I knew it I was enjoying the attention of men. Not long after that I began experimenting with one-night relationships. It was fun for a while, even though I knew it was wrong. But after a while I couldn't face myself in the mirror. Everything I was doing was against my values, my faith. I can look back now and see that I was trying to cover my pain with casual sex. It doesn't work."

It is so tempting to take the pain pill of sexual involvement. Who can blame us for looking for an escape from agony? But ultimately, the only true escape is *going through the grief with the Lord by your side.*

### Substance Abuse

Another common way to disguise grief is through the use of alcohol and other substances. Many who would not normally be prone to abusing substances fall prey to their allure to ease the pain when a relationship has ended. Many who normally would not be "bar-hoppers" find themselves vulnerable to the quick fix of numbness that accompanies substance abuse. Add the excitement of being sought after by a member of the opposite sex to a dose of alcohol and you have a potent mix.

This mix is especially dangerous to those who have "addictive personalities." Those with addictive personalities tend to go overboard with things that they become involved in. You probably know if this description fits you. If one drink automatically leads to two or three more, you must be extremely careful. What on the surface appears to be a little harmless relief can cause enormous havoc.

### Other Addictions

While many will try to fill their empty souls with substances, some will find other addictions to numb their sorrows. There are myriad ways to hide from grief. Some will use shopping or pornography while others will eat or gamble to escape the pain. In the end, however, the grief remains. Regardless of your attempts to deny it, the "hole in your soul" is still the problem.

## Embracing Grief

Thankfully, our Lord understands our grief and can identify with our struggles. The prophet Isaiah said that our Lord Jesus would be "despised and rejected by men, a man of sorrows, and familiar with suffering. Like one from whom men hide their faces he was despised, and we esteemed him not. Surely he took up our infirmities and carried our sorrows" (Isa. 53:3–4).

The methods for avoiding pain described in the previous section do not work, so what are we to do? Certainly we cannot face our weariness head on, can we? Actually, yes we can! Like the psalmist, we can cry aloud, "Turn to me and be gracious to me, for I am lonely and afflicted. The troubles of my heart have multiplied; free me from my anguish" (Ps. 25:16–17). And you can know that the Lord will honor these heart-rending pleas.

Meditate upon the powerful fact that Jesus has experienced all that we struggle with in this life. He has given us the gift of his Spirit to deal effectively with the challenges of the moment. His Spirit, or counselor, will come alongside us and be a balm to our seeping wounds. "I pray that out of his glorious riches he may strengthen you with power through his Spirit in your inner being" (Eph. 3:16). What a marvelous prayer and promise! With the help of the Spirit we can move through our season of pain.

Efforts to avoid the reality of your grief will be ineffective. You have been created in such a way that you will feel deeply hurt. Embrace that aspect of your personality.

As we embrace our grief and suffering we will find that one day we will wake up feeling better. We will slowly quit trying to fight the inevitable and come to that place, predicted by Kübler-Ross, called *acceptance.* We will say, "This *is* happening to me, and being angry and resentful about it will not change things." Working through our sadness and hurt *will* change things. It will deepen and strengthen us. When we accept what is happening, we can get on with deciding how to cope and how we want our lives to be as we go, or *grow,* through it.

Can you trust God to bring you through this difficult time? Yes, indeed you can.

## Summary

I close this chapter with the reminder that grief affects those who leave as well as those who are left behind. A commonly perpetuated myth about separation is that if you were the one to choose the separation, it will not be painful. Nothing could be further from the truth. In my work with those going through the trauma of lost love, I have been told clearly and poignantly by many people that even though they were the one who chose the separation, living through the experience is extremely difficult. Ginger tells her story:

"I lived with Jack for many years knowing that someday our marriage would end. I knew that I would be the one to end it because he would be willing to hang on forever. I tried living without sex for three years. I tried living with the knowledge that my husband was cheating on me, although I was never able to prove it. I knew that the church would disapprove when I left, yet I felt I had no other choice. When I left Jack, everyone was quick to ask me why I was leaving, as if I was doing something horrible. Because he didn't beat me or throw me around, I felt guilty for my choice. But I was losing myself more and more every year I stayed with him."

Ginger is experiencing a different aspect of the loss of separation. In addition to the anguish of being without the man she once loved, she faces the scrutiny of those who would sling arrows of shame at her. "How can you leave your husband?" they say. "Your decision seems selfish and unfounded." Her reason for leaving does not fit into the manual of right and wrong set forth by many churches.

Ginger and others like her suffer from rejection from those who criticize their actions. Instead of trying to understand Ginger's plight, they sling accusations at her when she needs understanding and acceptance. She will need to reach out carefully to those who can understand and will offer her comfort in her distress.

Those experiencing the confusion of lost love struggle to find their bearings. Their lives have been turned upside down. Let's explore now what it is like to face a life of uncertainty about what is going to happen next.

# 3

⟨⟨⟨◇◇◇◇◇◇◇◇◇◇◇◇◇◇◇◇◇◇⟩⟩⟩

# THE UNCERTAINTY
# OF WHAT'S NEXT

*Not everything that is faced can be
changed, but nothing can be changed
until it is faced.*

James Baldwin

L ife, for all its drama, consists mainly of connected routines. The predictability is comforting. Our routines
are like fences around our lives. We are secure behind the
wooden posts that keep us cordoned off from the unexpected until something, or someone, forces us to face life
beyond the borders of our comfortable world. Lost love tears

down these fences and compels us to confront dramatic changes. Sandy's story clearly illustrates the trauma of a broken relationship.

Sandy came home after a stressful day at the accounting firm where she worked as office manager to find her husband of twelve years, Todd, sitting solemnly at the kitchen table.

"Hello, Sandy," he said stiffly. "When you get settled I need to talk to you." Sandy noticed his serious demeanor and knew instantly that something was dreadfully wrong.

"What's wrong?" Sandy asked directly. "Are you all right?"

"I'm okay," he said slowly, avoiding her eyes. "But I'm not sure you will be after we talk. Why don't you go ahead and put your jacket away and come and sit down."

As Sandy hurried down the hall, her mind raced with the possible explanations for Todd's sober expression. They had been fighting more than usual about "typical issues"—children, finances, sex—but she doubted that could account for his mood.

"Well?" Sandy said, when she returned to the kitchen. "Let's have it. Is it anything I've done?"

"As a matter of fact," Todd said, "it does involve you, and us. I don't know how else to tell you this other than to just come out and say it: I'm not happy with our relationship and have decided to move out. I have been thinking about my feelings toward you and I don't think they are what they should be. I don't think I love you anymore."

Sandy stared at him in disbelief. She gasped for breath, heart pounding, as her mind struggled to process what she thought she had heard. Surely Todd wasn't saying that their marriage was over. Surely he was not willing to cast her aside for some dream of a better life.

"What are you saying?" Sandy asked incredulously. "Are you telling me that you want to end our marriage? You're really ready to give up on us?"

"No. I'm not ready to say that. I am just saying that I am really confused about my feelings. Some days I think I still love you and want to work on it. Some days I don't. We've talked about this in the past. You know how confused I've been."

"Confused, yes," she said, starting to cry, "but ready to move out? Isn't this a pretty extreme way to deal with a problem?"

Todd looked at her sympathetically. He seemed unwilling to thrust the knife of rejection in any further.

"I've been thinking about this for a long time," he said. "I've been . . . Well, I am moving out and may be filing for divorce. I've talked to an attorney. We can talk about it some more another time, but I will be leaving tonight. I want you and the kids to be alright. I'm not going to leave you high and dry. We'll talk about how to tell the kids later."

"Later?" Sandy shouted. "What do you mean later? This is happening right now. What do I tell them when they ask where you are? How do I explain why you're not here for them? We'll talk later? Just what do you expect me to do in the meantime?"

"I really am sorry, Sandy. I'm sure I don't look very good in your eyes right now. But I have to do this."

Sandy sat speechless. She began to feel numb, unsure of what to say or where to go. She feared what would happen next. She had never been through anything like this. She sat silently as Todd got up and left the house. She wondered how she would cope. What would she do now? When would he be coming back, and would he want to work on their relationship at all? Was she going to be left alone to raise their children? Thoughts and fears flooded her mind.

Sandy spent a restless night trying to digest what had happened that evening. Her emotions made it impossible to think straight. While their marriage was far from perfect, she did not want a separation or divorce. She was willing to do anything to work out their problems. They had spent many years together and divorce had been unthinkable. She wanted stability for herself and their children. But that was not what Todd wanted.

## Decisions

A thousand questions race through the minds of the one leaving and the one left behind. Decisions to end a relationship are never made easily or without incredible complications. A world is turned upside down. Routines are demolished. Safety is replaced by risk and fear. Sometimes one feels relief, but more often confusion and dread of what is coming next.

Because separation is so often one of the first major changes that occurs, let's consider some of the challenges facing the separating couple.

### Living Situations

When Todd walked out, Sandy was left with the family house. However, like most couples, they relied on two incomes to cover the monthly expenses. Now their incomes would be spread between two households rather than one.

Sandy walked around bewildered for the next few days. She struggled to sort out her deluge of feelings and cope with the hard choices facing her. Would she stay in the house? How could she afford to make payments? Todd had not called in days, and she was hesitant to call him. She dreaded the conversation about money she knew would follow. Would Todd be willing to help her while she determined whether it was feasible for her to remain in their home? Could they arrive at an equitable decision without becoming adversarial? And most of all, how could she remain calm when she wanted to choke him for abandoning her and their children?

If finances do not permit Sandy to stay, she will be faced with a new set of decisions: Where to live? What furniture and mementoes to take? What to do with the things that must be left? How to minimize the impact of moving on the children?

If Sandy is able to stay in the family home, cutbacks will surely have to be made. She also will be forced to deal with the emotions that are attached to the house. Memories of Todd and their life together will constantly invade the house and her heart.

When two people part, a ripple effect spreads in every direction. A change of residence for one of them is the initial step. Sometimes the move is as simple as carting belongings to an apartment complex down the block, but it may be as complicated as resettling in another city. In either case, the emotional impact can be monumental. Having to pack up your life and haul it to another location in a moving van can leave you feeling cold, empty, and exhausted.

You may have had to pack your life into U-Haul boxes, perhaps with the help of a few friends but most likely alone. Barely able to think, you had to sort through memories, wrap them in yesterday's news, and stuff them into cardboard boxes. You may have wept as you wondered what was to become of your life. All the while you wondered if there was still a chance to save the relationship.

Fragmented pieces of your life were strewn about in haphazard attempts at order. You labeled the boxes in the hope that doing so would make it easier to reassemble your life at the new location, but even worse, it would take much longer to put the pieces of your life back together. But you had to do it. You had to pull things together. Your kids' welfare depended on it; your job expected it of you; your personal well-being demanded it. Still, a life relegated to old things stuffed into worn-out boxes felt like no life at all. No matter how hard you tried to be strong, you couldn't stop the tears.

Lisa, another client going through a marital separation, told me of feeling discouraged and isolated as she waited in vain for her family to offer to help her move. Their lives were orderly, compressed, with little room for her crisis. She couldn't control the surging feeling of resentment as she moved, mostly by herself, manhandling things into the van by sheer determination. Her daughters could have helped, but she was trying to spare them from the harsh realities that lay ahead. They were staying with her parents for a few nights while she readied the place for their new life. She had considered hiring movers, but money would be tight in the days ahead. The reality of the life-altering event was beginning to sink in.

As she began unloading the boxes, Lisa became increasingly discouraged. Not being able to find the personal grooming items she needed that evening was the last straw. Tears flowed as she sat alone in the dark asking questions. Why was this happening? What was to become of her? Why didn't he love her anymore?

Like many others coping with lost love and the separation that often follows, Lisa felt like a vagabond when she moved. She had no real place to call home. Friends seemed distant, and potent emotions constantly reminded her that this was not a dream. Being alone had never felt this lonely.

Like many others, Lisa did not want to have to reach out for help. She was used to handling things on her own. She seemed proud that she had faced various crises in the past without "burdening others," as she called it. I encouraged her to swallow her pride and reach out to her support system. She had a strong network of caring friends who were more than willing to help if she asked.

If you are in this kind of situation, don't be afraid to ask for help. You cannot go through this devastating phase of your life alone. Consider all those whom you would call a friend and let them help you. Reach out, no matter how challenging it is to do so.

### Financial Considerations

Perhaps at the top of the list of immediate worries are those pertaining to money. In a world where finances are often stretched to the limit, money matters are a top stressor for any family. A separation often stretches family finances to a breaking point.

When Todd chose to leave the marriage and the family home, he too wondered how he would make ends meet. He planned to rent an apartment, but he did not want to settle for a ramshackle place in the low-rent district. He was used to having nice things and did not want to add insult to injury by living in a depressing place. Still, he knew he would need to pay Sandy monthly support payments for the children and help out with the mortgage until final decisions were made. This would leave him with more month than money, and he feared talking to Sandy about it. He couldn't expect her to be very sympathetic.

No one in a separation wants to suffer a demotion in lifestyle, but it is often inevitable. Typically one person stays in the family home, fretting about making the mortgage payment, while the other ends up in an apartment, reduced to a lifestyle they had long since left behind.

Deciding who will stay in the home and how to split up the family resources is often emotionally straining. The fact that one has been "left" and is reeling from rejection only adds to the emotional volatility of the situation. When there may still be hope of reconciliation, money matters further confound the situation and make healing more difficult.

### Children

Sandy and Todd had three children, ages three, five, and seven. They were too young to know the details of their parents' lost love or the steps leading to the separation. They were not too young, however, to know that Daddy would not be living with Mommy anymore. This raised several critical questions: How should the children be told? How much should they be told? How could they be told in a way that would minimize damage to them?

The pain of realizing that your children will not be raised in an intact family is excruciating. Most of us have an incredibly strong sense of loyalty and protection for our children and hate the thought that they will suffer. This is part of the emotional equation when a separation occurs. Children will be affected by the separation and ensuing relational and situational strain.

Children are often troubled as much by the months of conflict leading up to the separation as they are by the separation itself. The way parents handle this transition time is critical to the well-being of the children. A few tips on this transition may be helpful.

- Talk to them about what is happening each step of the way.
- Assure them that they are not to blame for the separation.
- Answer their questions honestly, avoiding unnecessary details.
- Assure them that they are loved and will be taken care of.
- Develop a parenting plan that gives children liberal access to both parents.
- Do not involve the children in struggles with the other parent.[1]

## Legal Considerations

Most couples going through a separation face the inevitable question of whether or not to involve an attorney. Suspicions grow as each wonders if the other has made a legal move. Sometimes, as in the case of Todd and Sandy, one partner has already made the decision. That leaves the other wondering if and when they should seek legal counsel.

One friend may quickly and emphatically tell you that your neck is on the line and you'd better get an attorney right away. Another friend, perhaps with a cooler disposition, may tell you that if you involve an attorney, things will get worse quickly. Good advice and easy solutions are hard to find.

You will need to be working toward a rational solution free from emotional outbursts. To help you, you will need to be cautious and seek out friends who seem to have good judgment and are free from their own issues and conflicts in the matter.

Perhaps the best step that can be taken initially is to take no action. It is best to move slowly, avoid adversarial positions, and pray about whether to seek legal advice. Prayer will not only help you to obtain wisdom, as Scripture promises, but also undoubtedly soften your heart and relieve some of your fear and anger. Time for reflection and consideration will help you discern what is best for you.

Few situations call for immediate action. While it may be tempting, as a result of feelings of hurt and revenge, to run to the sharpest attorney you can find, this is rarely the best course of action. Such sudden moves will not help the situation. The chance of reconciliation, which may be quite high, will likely be damaged by the involvement of an adversarial attorney.

If both partners have an attorney, the situation now usually takes on a "win-lose" tone. Each attorney is looking out for his client's welfare, as a lawyer should. However, their job is not to assist in the possible mending of the relationship. For this reason, use caution when considering hiring a lawyer, especially if you see hope for reconciliation. Maintain a conciliatory attitude even in the face of legalities. Try to remain open to what God may want to accomplish in your heart throughout this ordeal.

## Strategies for Sound Decision Making

You face so many decisions to be made that second-guessing yourself may become automatic. You will try to make rational decisions while your emotions are riding a roller coaster. You will wonder if you are making the right decision. Did you take enough time? Did you listen to the right people? The questions are endless and may seem like incoherent chatter in an already confused mind. Here are some strategies for clearing out the clutter and making the best decisions for your changing life.

### Seeking Stability

You have heard this said and it bears repeating: Keep things as simple as possible during these challenging times. Do not rush out to make major changes in your lifestyle. You need stability and routine. Guard your energy, reserving it to make critical decisions that cannot be avoided.

When one's world is turned upside down, things do not just fall into place again. While the world keeps spinning in its orbit and others' lives seem to continue humming along, you are left alone to catch up to the pace. You will need time to slow things down so that you can catch up. Even by simply remembering to inhale and exhale, you can help yourself feel normal again.

You should *reestablish routines as soon as possible*. The advice not to make unnecessary changes is wise counsel because you will have enough changes to reckon with without adding more to the heap. You may be surprised at how unsettled your life feels. A new living situation, legal and financial matters—all will demand your attention and energy.

When everything outside is shifting, maintain as much inner harmony as possible by renewing your intimacy with God. Some say that troubles are a spiritual elixir. When things in this world let us down, God is certainly always there to help us pick up the pieces. David, in the midst of terrible personal strife, exclaimed, "The LORD is my light and my salvation—whom shall I fear? The LORD is the stronghold of my life—of whom shall I be afraid?" (Ps. 27:1). With predators on every side, he chose to focus on the Lord. We would be well advised to do the same.

We live hectic lives with little room for crisis. When one comes, it can be devastating. Crises take an emotional toll that consumes our energy. Fear about what is coming next can drain every ounce of strength. Strangely, you may not be aware of how you are losing your energy, only that you are dead tired at the end of your day. "Why am I so exhausted?" you wonder.

Because of the emotional drain, *this is a time to conserve energy by taking good care of yourself.* You will likely need extra rest. Getting plenty of sleep, eating healthy foods, taking vitamins, and getting that winter flu shot are simple ways to enhance your flagging immune system. Making sure to set good boundaries by saying "no" and "yes" to demands appropriately will also help. When you make a decision, think carefully about the implications of the choice. Ask yourself, "Is this decision good for me? How will it impact me? How will it ultimately impact others?"

### Seeking Time and Space for Restoration

In addition to keeping things simple and conserving energy, you will need to give yourself lots of time. Said simply, go slowly. Give yourself space to think things through. Decisions will come more easily if you have given yourself quiet time to ponder them.

Studies are replete with examples of the importance of sleep to our restoration. Sleep is a special kind of "time and space." Dr. Anthony Storr, the renowned psychiatrist and author, says,

> When faced with a problem to which there is no obvious answer, conventional wisdom recommends "sleeping on it," and conventional wisdom is right. Most people have had the experience of being unable to make up their minds when faced with a difficult decision, and of going to bed with the decision still not made. On waking in the morning they often find that the solution has become so obvious that they cannot understand why they could not perceive it on the previous night. Some kind of scanning and re-ordering

process has taken place during sleep, although the exact nature of this process remains mysterious.[2]

Dr. Storr goes on to talk about the importance of solitude to the restoration process. He denounces the "noise" of our society, explaining that it can be especially damaging for those who are going through a mourning process. He encourages us to remove ourselves from the sights and sounds that would distract us from the task at hand: considering our losses. He says, "Removing oneself voluntarily from one's habitual environment promotes self-understanding and contact with the inner depths of being which elude one in the hurly-burly of day to day life."[3]

In Western society we do not give much credence to solitude, but I assure you that it is necessary and beneficial. Over the past ten years or so, I have developed a practice of going away to a retreat center for a weekend of prayer and silence. I remember clearly how frightened I was the first time I left behind family and friends, not to mention Starbucks and cable television, and drove to this wooded monastery. As I approached the shrub-lined drive to the estate, I was nervous. Gone was the cloak of my comfortable routine.

I was greeted cordially but with obvious reserve. The nun had a ready smile but was not chatty. That was my first brush with the graciousness of simplicity. It was refreshing. She made it clear that she was available for any need but would not be intrusive. *She knew that both time and space were important for restoration.*

When I walked into my room, I found no framed pictures, comfortable chairs, stereo system, or television. The austere room was designed for reflection and solitude, being alone with yourself and God. But what a delight those times away from outside responsibilities have come to be!

Although I recommend this experience, I know that it is not for everyone. Perhaps you will be more comfortable with twenty or thirty minutes of daily meditation or contemplation. A daily time of prayer spent listening to God can create a space in which to be rebalanced and restored in spirit.

### Seeking Information

I recently took a trip to Italy with my youngest son. We had a wonderful time, but we also felt frustrated because we could not speak the language or understand the customs. Rich cultural experiences and growth could have been ours had we done more to prepare and educate ourselves. Imagine asking for directions or information about the history of a place from an Italian who could not speak English, using only an Italian phrasebook.

When we leave the land of the married and enter the land of the separated, we are similarly handicapped. We are left standing helplessly by the side of the road, trying to understand the hieroglyphics on the signs. Sadly, we have few guides along the way offering assistance. We do not know what is happening to us or what is going to happen next. What will become of us? Who will come to our rescue?

To develop a surer footing, you must ask for directions. Help can come in several different forms. Look for programs that offer special assistance to those struggling with separation. For example, churches sometimes offer classes for those in transition. Depending on your circumstances, you may also feel accepted in a divorce recovery group.

Few feelings are as painful as feeling isolated and alone in your experience. Thus you have a critical need for others who can relate to what you are going through. While you may not find a perfect fit, look for those who have experienced separation and perhaps divorce.

### Seeking Counsel

In addition to seeking information, seek godly counsel. You will probably find that many are willing to offer their advice on what you should be doing with your life. Everyone seems to have an opinion, and if you listen to them all, you will end up going in circles. The plethora of opinions means that not everyone can be right. But deciphering who is right and who is wrong can be a daunting task. Determining who best understands your unique circumstances and your unique value system is essential. Find someone who resonates with your spirit. You will know you have found that person when your spirit feels "at home." The following markers will assist you in determining whose counsel is genuinely godly advice:

1. How do you feel about the person offering the advice? Do you connect with him or her?
2. Does their counsel square up with Scripture? Do they offer biblical principles that support their counsel?
3. As you listen to their counsel, do you feel a sense of peace? Godly counsel will leave you with *clarification, confirmation,* and *peace.*
4. Are you able to be honest with this person? Sharing with them does no good if you feel you have to put on a mask. Do they accept you for who you are, warts and all?

This difficult path will be easier if you can travel with a companion who accepts you for what you are and where you are on your journey. Ask God to send mentors who will assist you in the journey.

### Seeking Community

During this challenging time, nothing can take the place of a caring community. I cannot emphasize enough the importance of being surrounded by friends and family members with whom you can be honest. You will need several people to serve as the legs of your stool by listening to your anger, confusion, and sadness.

Because you will be "needy" during these challenging days, don't be surprised if you "wear out" one or two of the legs at times. You will likely need several people willing to walk with you through this valley.

I have belonged to a men's group for years. It was formed as a place to be supportive of one another. It is a weekly time when I can share my sorrows, struggles, and accomplishments. The group members help me with decisions, and I know they will not judge me. Because we all struggle with similar issues, we find great freedom in this atmosphere. I am not alone because we share our strengths and weaknesses, our hopes and fears. Such a group can be a profoundly healing environment for you in times of struggle like you are facing now.

### Seeking God

We seek God when we are lost and in need of direction because God knows our hearts and knows what is best for us. Our friends can provide support, but surely all of our decisions need to be bathed in prayer.

Does God care about even the little decisions in our lives? Of course. The Scriptures remind us, "Look at the birds of the air; they do not sow or reap or store away in barns, and yet your heavenly Father feeds them. Are you not more valuable than they?" (Matt. 6:26).

Besides gaining counsel and wisdom from our heavenly Father, in prayer we are offered *peace in the midst of the storm.* God promises to walk through the valleys with us. The prophet Isaiah reminds us of God's constant protection while we are under fire from adversity:

> So do not fear, for I am with you;
>   do not be dismayed, for I am your God.
> I will strengthen you and help you;
>   I will uphold you with my righteous right
>   hand. . . .
> For I am the LORD, your God,
>   who takes hold of your right hand
> and says to you, Do not fear;
>   I will help you.
>
> Isaiah 41:10, 13

As you encounter the darkest days of your life and feel abandoned by those you counted on to be there for you, remember that the One who will never leave you or forsake you is a prayer away. You can reach out to him right now.

Dear Jesus, I pray that you come close to me now, in the middle of my dark hours, and comfort me. I pray for your peace that passes understanding. At a time when I have lost love and am confused, I call upon you to help me with the decisions that bombard me. Help me find the wisdom that you offer so generously. Amen.

## Summary

Separation is a tumultuous event. Even for those who seek a separation and find relief in it, it is still a disquieting situation. As the old routines evaporate along with a way of life we have enjoyed, we are left to create a new life. Nearly everything changes, and it is easy to fall prey to fear. The uncertainty of what's coming next can paralyze us.

The antidote to fear is courage, and this is a time to muster all you can. This is a time to use your courage to embrace any routines still intact and establish new routines where necessary. Call old friends for support. Force yourself to go to work and pride yourself in work well done. Make time for prayer and journaling, reflecting on what is happening to you—finding meaning in any tragedy makes suffering bearable. Take care of yourself by exercising regularly and eating right. Above all else, give special care to your children.

The struggles that accompany a broken relationship cannot be avoided. They must, in fact, be embraced. There is no way around them, nor can we effectively deny them. The temptation to use any number of numbing devices must be avoided as well. We must squarely face our pain. If we do that, we will come out on the other side stronger than ever.

# 4

<><><><><><><><><><><><><><><><><><><><><>

# VULNERABILITY

*My hope, my grief, my loss, my love,*
*Did all within this circle move.*

Edmund Waller

The summer months bring a respite from the bitter cold and biting rain here in the Pacific Northwest. We turn up the collars on our raincoats from November until March, but even when April arrives we wait anxiously for the daily weather predictions.

But the welcome warmth of summer brings unwanted risks. Many days without precipitation during July, August, and September create a tinderbox effect, and our luxuriant forests are vulnerable. As I write this chapter, thousands of acres of forest are burning, the result of a fire started by a single lightning bolt.

While most Northwesterners are delighted to see another day without rain, firefighters stand ready for word that another blaze has erupted. Summer will not be a time for vacation for them; they will work fourteen-hour shifts seven days a week until the long-awaited rains arrive.

Losing acres of Douglas fir and Sitka spruce to an act of nature is one thing. Losing it to a carelessly tossed cigarette or an abandoned campfire is quite another. The tiniest ember can cause millions of dollars of damage and demolish thousands of acres of mature forest.

If you have suffered the effects of lost love, you may be thinking of the careless spark of passion or unrestrained emotion that created the blaze that devastated your life. The truth is, our relationships are often as vulnerable as a tinder-dry forest. Not possible, you say? Think again.

**The Emptiness of Love Lost**

When a man or woman is told that they are no longer loved, a vacuum replaces the security of commitment. Each morning you rise alone—emotionally, physically, or both. Everything you counted on to provide structure and comfort in your life is gone. Love lost is a frightening land, where fear creates its own limits to living.

Love lost often leads to marital separation, because the vacuum it creates cannot tolerate even the semblance of intimacy. The brokenness, tumult, and devastation that result must not be understated. The toll they take on our personal well-being is usually enormous.

In this vacuum—the precious space once reserved for and occupied by warmth and generosity—love lost often creates a fearful unpredictability. The unwelcome stranger may be feelings of darkness and uncertainty that you have not known for years. Some of the difficulties of this fearful unpredictability can be managed; many, however, must simply be endured. In the meantime, you feel incredibly vulnerable. Raw emotions surge just below the surface, like the swelling of ocean waves before a storm, ready to erupt at a moment's notice. You struggle in rage, sadness, hurt, and fear. And that fear can be extreme at times. *What is to become of me?* you wonder.

Blistered, bruised, and hurting, you may look for any port in the storm. With self-recriminations echoing within you, hearing a soothing voice is so comforting. Without knowing it, you are vulnerable to the danger of accepting comfort and solace from people and behaviors which you might avoid under more stable conditions.

For some, the opposite may occur. Feeling betrayed, you may run from any offer of closeness or support. Your wounds are so bare, so sensitive to the touch, that you perceive every suggestion or offer of help as criticism. This too is a form of vulnerability.

## Vulnerability Defined

As you attempt to work through this transitional time of love lost, people will warn you about the dangers of vulnerability. At times these warnings may be welcome; at other times they may feel abrasive. Exactly what are people talking about when they dole out these warnings? What is this mysterious disease called *vulnerability* that you have contracted?

Think of vulnerability as a set of attitudes and feelings experienced after a significant loss. This is an unsettled time of rampant emotions and confused thinking during which you are uncertain about yourself and what you are experiencing. You have lost your bearings and are cast adrift. Self-doubt seems inescapable.

Because you are caught up in a whirlpool of emotions such as anger, hurt, rejection, and sadness, you cannot attend effectively to what is happening at the moment. You may feel dazed, unable to concentrate. You may be interacting with people, events, and emotions in the present while also reacting to events and people from your past. Hypersensitive to criticism, you may perceive the best-intended advice as rejection. *In short, you are fragile.* This fragility is vulnerability.

This period of vulnerability is also fraught with *triggers*. Triggers are events or words that reawaken past experiences. You may be driving and hear the song you used to sing with your partner. You may see the same model car he or she drives—and suddenly all of your senses are on red alert. "Watch out," they seem to say, "or you will be flooded with pain again." It is important to anticipate the triggers. Sometimes the best thing you can do is prepare for them, giving yourself time and space to grieve again. Call a friend to share the experience, or simply notice the feeling and move forward in your day.

Vulnerability is not something to be avoided. In fact, you cannot help but be vulnerable. You cannot stem the tide of your emotions. Being vulnerable is not a judgment of your value. You do not need to feel ashamed of feeling vulnerable because it happens to every person in the throes of change.

## Remembering Grief

As we have discussed in a previous chapter, love lost typically creates monumental grief. That grief is part of what makes many people so vulnerable. Their emotions are caught in a series of roller coaster cycles, one day up, the next day down. One morning the world seems manageable, while the next day you may feel caught in sadness and despair. At times you may feel like you are losing your mind. Not to worry. This is how grief feels, but it will come to an end. In the meantime, you have decisions to be made and life to be lived. Life does not stop because you are having a crisis.

The important question is, How are you doing emotionally? Have you given yourself time to understand your emotional swings? Have you engaged all the legs of your stool so that trusted friends support you? Have you taken care of the business of your marriage so that it is not clouding other friendships?

Your immediate task is to *manage your grief and deal with your marriage.* Although you may be tempted to move into another relationship or to run from your pain, avoid those lures. *Each stage of separation has its own challenges and emotions to master.*

## Embracing Vulnerability

I have emphasized the importance of "being with" the feelings you are experiencing at a particular moment. Do not try to deny your vulnerability or label it as "bad." Embracing your pain is possible. Meanwhile, you can learn to be kind to yourself and to pamper yourself toward healing.

In sharing the gut-wrenching loss of his father, Michael Downey talks about vulnerability. In an article titled "Brief Gold," he writes,

> Vulnerability is often thought to refer to a weakness that places us in a position of being forced to give in indiscriminately to any and all powers and forces. It is often thought that vulnerability causes us to be adversely affected by persons, events, and circumstances beyond our control. . . . Properly understood, however, the term describes the fundamental openness of the human being to be affected by life, persons, and events. To be human is to be vulnerable, indeed defenseless, in the face of so many of the events and persons that touch us, for good or ill. At the most fundamental level, human vulnerability is part and parcel of being a person, having a body, being embodied.[1]

Vulnerability, according to Downey, is not something we can avoid if we are willing to be human. If we are willing to be genuinely touched by others, we face the risk of pain. We can choose to wall ourselves off from others and even from God, but that is a tall price to pay for safety. It is a bit like plodding along encased in armor, hoping to avoid skinning your knees.

Separation will bring times of extreme tenderness. Times of tears, fears, hurts, and shadowy hopes. Questions will flood your mind, making sleep impossible. But there is at least one thing you have the power to do at these moments: *embrace your vulnerability.* You feel because you are alive, and for that reason you can allow God to touch you in new and deeper ways than you have known before.

> *It is better to learn early of the inevitable depths, for then sorrow and death take their proper place in life, and one is not afraid.*
>
> Pearl S. Buck

### Identifying Your Needs

During this time of vulnerability you will be needy. I do not mean that in a derogatory sense. I intend it purely as a factual statement. As I have illustrated, you will feel like you are on a nonstop roller coaster ride that leaves you breathless and exhausted. This roller coaster ride is common to those going through the incredible pain of love lost, and some of its turns are predictable. One is that you will have increased needs, and you will often be particularly sensitive to having those needs met.

I remember someone saying to me after a relationship ended that they felt like they had a sign on their forehead that read, "I'm Needy, what's your name?" This may be a bit exaggerated, but there is certainly more than a grain of truth to their statement.

Let's explore some of the needs that rise to the surface when we are reeling from the effects of lost love.

### A Need for Self-Esteem

We all need to feel important to others and worthwhile as individuals. If you have felt rejected in some way in your primary relationship, your self-esteem has probably been bruised. You may feel guilt-ridden over your inability to make the relationship work. You may feel deflated and humiliated if your spouse has rejected you. The love you once shared is gone. If a separation has not yet happened, you may fear that it will. You have undoubtedly been plagued with questions such as *What is so wrong with me that would make someone leave me?*

This time of painful rejection can also be a time of great self-reflection and learning. Dorothy Briggs, author of *Celebrate Yourself,* challenges us in this, saying, "The time when rejection's sting becomes unbearable is when it joins with our own self-rejection. If each rejection cuts you to the bone, you need to look at why you are rejecting yourself."[2]

At the very time when you are experiencing painful rejection by another, Briggs suggests, you may also be rejecting yourself. Painful as it is, this insight is important to understand. It can lead you to view yourself, and your partner, in new and helpful ways.

People tend to be overly critical of themselves. We are tempted to try to be "perfect." The perfectionist's voice, which you may have carried with you for a long time, will constantly criticize you. This criticism is bound to erode your feelings of self-worth. We need to remember that our value is not derived from being a good wife or husband, as imperative as that is. Our value comes from being exactly who our Creator created us to be.

After being bombarded with the news of love lost along with intense feelings of rejection and loss, you may find the excitement of a new attraction thrilling. At these moments we are like seeping wounds in need of a bandage. Finding someone who actually likes us, warts and all, can be addictive. "Wow!" we say. "Here is someone who wants more of my time, not less. Here is someone who wants to be with me, not reject me." But be careful not to overstate the significance of a new relationship. The attraction may be wonderful, but it is usually not love. It is probably an attempt to make yourself feel valued, and if you are not careful it could end in even more hurt.

### A Need to Accept Our True Selves

Closely related to the need for self-esteem is the need to accept our true selves. During times of rejection and loss, we come face-to-face with our core self. We see, in vivid detail, what makes us tick. Sometimes it is not a pretty sight.

Stop for a moment and think about how loss of love (and possibly marital separation) has affected you. To determine what this loss has taught you about yourself, consider the following questions:

- Have I found it easy to reach out to others when lonely?
- What have I learned about my self-concept?
- Have I been able to be comfortable alone with myself?
- Have I found myself able to reach out to God?

- Have I been able to trust that God is in control of my life?
- What new aspects of myself have I discovered during this crisis?

Although painful, this time in the crucible of rejection can be a refining fire. It can be a time when you come face-to-face with some of your deepest longings and fears. You may discover old fears that you thought were gone. This can be a time of teaching like no other. Solomon tells us, "When times are good, be happy; but when times are bad, consider: God has made the one as well as the other" (Eccles. 7:14). We can use these times as opportunities to look at the direction of our lives, at our values, and at our priorities.

Crises and transition can be fruitful times of understanding. Many of the routines that gave structure to your life are gone, and you stand face-to-face with yourself. This is a time when you can look in a mirror and consider who you really are on your own. Have you defined yourself with the prop of being a husband or a wife? Have you derived your identity solely from being loved by your spouse? Now you must look deeper and higher for new ways of defining yourself. If you do so, this time of vulnerability can be profoundly vital in redefining yourself.

### A Need for Comfort

During this disquieting period, you will probably feel a need to be soothed and comforted. In many ways you may feel like you are regressing, longing to go back home to your parents, to the family that will care for you. These feelings are perfectly natural in your current circumstances.

However, what you do with these feelings will be of critical importance to your healing.

You may seek comfort from a ready ear only to find that there are hidden or not-so-hidden strings attached. One lonely person seeking comfort often finds another lonely person needing comfort. But be careful—this type of seemingly innocent encounter can hold the seeds of disaster. Many have gone before you on this path and discovered later, after having their heart broken again, that a fog of vulnerability clouded their vision. Guard your heart, for it cannot easily withstand being broken again. You will always find those who will listen to you, but if they have a secondary agenda—especially romantic entanglement—beware!

So what should you do when you have such a strong need for comfort? Where do you turn when you hurt so badly yet are tired of calling on the same friends or family members for support?

Your raw pain needs soothing, to be sure. With some searching and sensitivity, you will find others, preferably of the same sex, who can comfort you during this time of need. As you pray for comfort, the Lord will bring people to you who can offer true friendship. This will require, however, that you exercise discretion in reaching out to others who are safe for you. This is not the time for romance!

Let's consider what to look for in a "safe friend."

- Someone who has no ulterior motive in your friendship.
- Someone who can keep confidences.
- Someone who will not malign your spouse.

- Someone who will be truthful with you.
- Someone who has demonstrated godly wisdom.
- Someone skilled at active listening.
- Someone without a need to tell you what to do.
- Someone who has demonstrated shared values.
- Someone who has the necessary time to be your friend.

### A Need to Be Touched

One of my fondest childhood memories is of my father playing "pig pile" with us kids. He challenged us to jump on his back and try to get the best of him. He let us believe that it was possible for us to win this "battle," and we were always up for the challenge. I can remember his huge frame, his hairy chest and back, and his large hands that gleefully tickled us. Most of all I remember his touch. It felt good—so good, in fact, that I passed the game on to my two sons when they were small. I hope they have the same kind of fond memories.

We must not underestimate the powerful urge within us to be touched. We long to be close to someone, to be in physical and emotional contact with them. We were created to be in relationships. God said at creation that it was not good for man to be alone (Gen. 2:18). We should not be surprised, then, to feel after separation a longing to be held, comforted, and, yes, touched.

Sidney Simon, in an article titled "Caring, Feeling, Touching," states, "There is a deep-seated hunger within us that no amount of food can satisfy. It is a hunger for touch, the feel, the concrete reality of human contact. Quite literally, it is 'skin hunger.' "[3] This desire to be touched is innate, primitive. We have it as children, and it remains, despite our beliefs to the contrary, until death.

The events leading up to the declaration that love has been lost undoubtedly included a decline of touch. During those months or perhaps years, you felt the cold rejection taking place. Perhaps it was gradual; perhaps it happened almost overnight. Perhaps you denied it for a long time. You knew, however, that the warmth of physical touch was leaving the relationship. For some people this loss is more painful and damaging than any other.

Sadly, many of us have ignored this need for touch and thus hunger for it. After a significant loss, the need seems to intensify. We are hungry for skin contact and may look for it in ways that are counter-therapeutic. Here again you are vulnerable. When you need to be touched, even something as innocent as a warm handshake can send tingles up your spine. Better yet is the sensual delight of sitting next to someone who is listening to you and perhaps reaching for your hand. Proceed with caution. The need to be touched can overpower your rationality. It is better, if not as exciting, to meet your need for touch through hugs, handshakes, and backslaps from safe, same-sex friends.

## The Dangers of Vulnerability

Now that we have made it clear that vulnerability is natural and not something to be avoided, we must look at some of the dangers that may accompany it. These are pitfalls we can avoid if we know they are in the road ahead. Let's examine a few of them.

### Indiscriminate Trust

Filled with confusing thoughts and emotions, you may be tempted to tell your story to anyone who listens. With many ready to listen and wanting to give advice, it can be very enticing to talk and talk and talk to anyone willing to listen.

But not so fast. All too soon you will find that the plethora of advice feels like an avalanche cascading over you. What do you do with the conflicting advice? Won't your friends be disappointed if you don't follow their counsel? Whose advice is right for you?

Henri Nouwen, the famed theologian and author, talks about vulnerability in the presence of someone you love and care about: "In the presence of people you love, your needs grow and grow, until those people are so overwhelmed by your needs that they are practically forced to leave you for their own survival."[4]

The solution lies in being careful. Ensure that you are careful in selecting those you trust with the intimate details of your life. Search for the right balance of sharing and avoid too much disclosure. Personal sharing involves timing—learning to share bits of information after you have deemed the person to be trustworthy and helpful. You do not want your personal life to be fodder for those who have little else to talk about. Remember that "a gossip separates close friends" (Prov. 16:28).

### Sudden Decisions

Because this is a time of extreme emotions and extreme confusion, decisions are often hard to make. Yet you will be tempted to make radical decisions to quickly end the pain—as if you could cut off your arm to get your throbbing wrist to quit hurting. But we dare not dismember ourselves. We dare not cut off parts of our past just because they contain painful memories.

This is a time of instability and change. You cannot know what tomorrow will hold, because you are in the gap between distinct worlds. You are in severe conflict with your spouse; you may be considering a separation; you are neither divorced nor happily married. In this confusing space, it is often best to take things slow and easy. Rushed decisions rarely turn out well.

You may be tempted to make a rash decision regarding where to live. Instead, be patient. You may want to take quick legal action. Hold off. You may want to quit your job and make a sudden career move. Wait. You may want to run into the arms of that caring friend of the opposite sex. Give it time. With all the enticements you face, be cautious. Slow down. Consider carefully. Your world is changing, and you will see things differently in time.

> *The sun shines so cold, so cold, when there are no eyes to look love on me.*
>
> George Eliot

John waited. His wife had left him two months earlier, and he felt desperately lonely. Yet he resisted the temptation to rush out and make friends indiscriminately. It was not easy, but he chose to go through the challenge of spending time alone and with a few male friends. He shared his story with me.

"The first few weeks were horrible. I didn't know what to do with myself. I wanted to call Lisa every minute of the day.

But I knew that she needed time, and I needed to learn to be alone with myself. I believed things would get better, and they did. I learned to spend time alone and devoted more hours to prayer and Bible study. I was active in my church. I connected with several guys who enjoy running, like I do. And I tried to deepen myself. I wanted to learn how to cook, so I bought some magazines and started practicing. After a while, the loneliness lessened and I began to feel more at ease. It all takes time."

### Lack of Support

While you must be careful in deciding whom to confide in, you do need support. You cannot go through this crisis alone. Most of the countless people I have counseled through this difficulty feel isolated and alone. Most try to make it through with the help of only one or two friends. In my experience that is not enough. However, *carefully choosing safe friends* is critical.

Nothing will make this time more challenging than facing it in isolation. Sitting alone in your apartment or home mulling your plight will amplify painful emotions. These conditions make it hard to keep things in perspective and make sound decisions. We need friends and wise, godly counsel.

Remember the example of the stool. Our friends and perhaps family members can provide the legs to the stool that will keep us up. At times one friend may not be available, while another may be. You will need to gauge your resources and use them wisely.

### Early Romances

So here you are, feeling incomplete, confused, and hurting, wanting some semblance of normalcy back in your life. You don't know what your future holds, and you are starting to doubt that all will be fine.

In this vortex of bewilderment and swollen emotions, you may be subconsciously looking for someone who will really understand. In these circumstances, fast romances often occur. Let's listen as Susan tells her story.

"I had been separated for about four months. It didn't look good for Dale and me, but we were just letting some time pass before we made any definite decisions. I was not looking for any new relationship. But I was terribly lonely and wondered how I was going to handle this shaky time in our relationship. What happened surprised even me.

"I had been working as an office manager. Most of my co-workers were men. I had been there for years, and the guys treated me like their sister. But as soon as they knew I was separated, something seemed to change. I don't know if it was me or them. It seemed like they all wanted to talk to me and were willing to listen as I cried and told them how horrible my life was. During our breaks and after work, I began meeting with one man in particular. Before I knew it, I was starting to have feelings for him. He was easy to talk to, whereas my husband had been so cold and angry.

"Before I knew it, I was developing romantic feelings for this man. I knew in my heart that it wasn't right, but I felt so vulnerable. I wanted to be understood and to be told that I was pretty. He said all the things I had wished my husband would say. Since my husband was rejecting me, I decided it was all right to have a relationship, even though I knew in my heart it was the wrong thing to do.

"This man and I had a hot and heavy romance for about six weeks. But it didn't take long for me to see that this was not someone I wanted to spend my life with or to be a father to my children. He just came along at the right time, and I was tempted to fall in love. But it wasn't love. I see that now. I just needed to be touched, to be understood, to be found attractive."

Susan's story is common. Men and women who are going through a transition have needs and often look to a quick romance to meet those needs. Sadly, most end up in more disappointment and bitterness. Raw wounds from the marital separation are opened again with fresh pain and hurt. Unfortunately, it then takes even longer to come to terms with the marital separation.

### A Need to Be Understood

If you are caught in the throes of lost love and the changes that come with a broken marriage, you will need help making sense out of the rampant emotions swirling about inside you. *What is going on inside me?* you may wonder. *Why do I have all of these conflicting thoughts and ideas? Why do I want to pull my mate closer, even though I was the one who was rejected? Why do I want to see my spouse hurt like I am hurting?*

You want to understand yourself and be understood. These desires make you vulnerable. Without intending to, you will have your radar out for anyone willing to listen to you. A colleague may ask how you are and before you know it you will have given them a twenty-minute rendition of your life. The words seem to spill out of you onto whoever seems emotionally available.

The need to be understood and to share your story is real. Find safe places where you can share what you are experiencing without fear of rejection, criticism, or romantic connections.

## Vulnerability and Attachment

Vulnerability and attachment are, of course, inextricably linked. The more attached we are to someone (or something), the more we suffer when we lose them, whether through a broken relationship or death. If we care about someone with any kind of depth and selflessness, we will have anguish at the loss.

Does that mean we should then quit caring about others and avoid any kind of attachment? Of course not. Love has its risks, and they are worth it. But we would do well to keep in the back of our minds that our loved ones are only on loan to us; they will leave us, or we will leave them, at some time.

The words of Christ found in the Gospel of Matthew are appropriate here. Consider his words: "Do not store up for yourselves treasures on earth, where moth and rust destroy, and where thieves break in and steal. But store up for yourselves treasures in heaven, where moth and rust do not destroy, and where thieves do not break in and steal. For where your treasure is, there your heart will be also" (Matt. 6:19–21). We must keep our attachments in perspective, including our loved ones.

## Dealing Effectively with Vulnerability

We have listed many of the traits along with some of the dangers of vulnerability. Now let's look at strategies for dealing constructively with these confusing emotions.

First, *honor this season of tenderness in your life.* See your current circumstances as a season that will not last forever. You will, in all likelihood, move through the stages of grief and on to a wonderful celebration of a new life. This new life may be a renewal of your love relationship with your spouse. It may be a new season of being alone in which you can deepen your relationship with God, others, and yourself. Begin by setting this time aside as a season of learning.

Second, *be gentle with yourself.* You are fragile and need extra TLC. You can attend to your own wounds by making choices that will contribute to healing. You can take extra care in the foods you eat, the way you treat your body, and the activities you engage in. Hot baths, scented candles, and nourishing meals are just a few of the simple pleasures that can renew your energies.

Third, *reach out for appropriate support.* You do not need to, nor should you, go through this storm alone. You need healthy friendships to navigate these difficult waters. Take care to find wise, godly counsel to help you make good decisions for you and your marriage.

Fourth, *set healthy boundaries.* This means everything from choosing healthy friends to determining how much you will tell them. It means not letting any unhealthy people into your life. It means making deliberate choices that set you on the road to recovery. Anything you do to short circuit your pain will only prolong your difficulties.

Fifth, *give to others from the storehouse of God's gifts to you.* A crisis is often a very fruitful time for exploring untapped creative potential. Volunteer your time to some charitable organization; support others in their struggles by listening with an open heart; find an outlet for your creative abilities.

Finally, *rest in the Lord.* While this may sound like just another trite religious cliché, God promises us peace in the midst of our trials. He does not promise to take away the pain, but he does promise to be present with us in the midst of the pain. C. S. Lewis said that joy is not the absence of pain but God's presence in the midst of the pain. Asking for God's help is an essential step in dealing with your personal tragedy.

## Summary

We have been dealing with the cold nakedness that comes from lost love. Perhaps the most important thing to remember during this sensitive time is that it will not last. That knowledge will give you hope. This is a phase, a season that will resolve itself in due time. Sadly, you cannot speed it up or move through it faster. The myriad decisions you face will require time to settle before you determine what step to take next. But, in time, you will discover the right direction for your life.

Loving and risking attachment to others always involves great risks. Don't we wish it were not so! Most of the time we comfort ourselves within feelings of invulnerability when at some level we know it is not so. Love lost crashes through the membrane of invulnerability and brings us to our knees.

Love lost reminds us of the incredible fragility of life. It reminds us that love, with all of its greatness, can sometimes
be taken away abruptly. The challenge for each of us is to
simply love and to work hard to preserve love's integrity,
being aware that we control precious little in this life.

There are ways to manage the roller coaster ride of broken
love, which we will discuss in the next chapter.

# 5

## THE RIDE

*There is a time for departure even*
*when there is no place to go.*

Tennessee Williams

Tad awakened early to a crisp March morning, the sun bursting through his eastern window. Startled, he glanced at the clock on his nightstand to be sure that he was not late for work. He had time to snooze for a change.

As the fog of sleep lifted, he realized that the days must be getting longer. Perhaps the mornings would be filled with light. He cheerily readied himself for work. In front of the mirror he noted that he looked happier. He wondered if this might be a sign that he was beginning to recover from his separation. Eleven months ago he had been told that he was no longer loved by a wife who said she needed her "space." It had been a long year.

As he lathered his face for his morning shave, the phone rang. He wiped off the lather and rushed to the phone.

"Hi, Tad," the voice on the other end of the line said softly.

Tad didn't recognize the voice at first. "Who is this?"

"It's Bev. How are you?"

He hadn't heard this voice in six months. His wife had left him nearly a year ago in order to "find herself." They had talked for a time after the separation, but their discussions were filled with tension and bitterness. Tad could not understand her reason for leaving, and she had refused to go to counseling. They had been moving inexorably toward the divorce that would be final within the next month.

"Why are you calling?" Tad said, feeling suddenly frightened. He was confused as to why she might be calling, especially this early in the morning. Just talking to her could trigger a groundswell of emotions.

"I'm not sure why I'm calling," Bev said. She seemed to be measuring her words carefully. "I just thought that maybe we could get together and talk. What do you think about that?"

"You can't be serious, Bev," Tad said. His irritation surprised him. "I haven't heard from you in six months, and you call me out of the blue and say you want to talk. What am I supposed to think?"

Bev had not expected a cheery greeting, but she was not prepared for this unfriendliness from Tad. After a few moments of silence she spoke.

"I can understand that I've caught you off guard. But I'd like to talk. Why don't we get together for a cup of coffee and catch up with each other?"

"Look, Bev, I hate to be rude, but I'm just starting to get my life back in some kind of order. The last year has been hell on me. I'm not real excited about jumping back on the ferris wheel with you. Let me think about it, and I'll call you in a few days."

"That's fine," she said in her controlled voice. "No demands. No expectations. Just some talking. Give me a call after you've had a chance to think about it."

## On Again, Off Again

Unfortunately, the road from lost love to separation and either divorce or reconciliation is rarely a straight one. Rather than a smooth, linear highway, it is often a neglected back road filled with bumps and potholes, twists and turns. The result can be brutal to our mental health during a time when we yearn for stability.

When you leave the predictable world of marriage for the world of lost love and possible separation, you may feel like an icy glass of water has been thrown in your face. The uncertainties that follow can be numbing. You will be best off if you brace yourself for a series of painful events. You should also anticipate that things can go awry when least expected. Though you can try to prepare yourself for your future, your spouse has a very large say in how things turn out. Many rightly say that we can only control our actions and reactions, not those of our partner. Understanding and preparation are two invaluable keys to successfully handling a troubled relationship.

I have never seen a relationship come apart in one swift action. They unravel like a frayed rope, strand by failing strand. One does not take the relational rope and simply snip it apart, as much as one may wish to do so at times. Rather, the band tying us to our partner is gradually torn. Each memory, each experience, is a strand in the fraying relational rope. Both partners incur some emotional tearing when a love relationship reaches an end. If a separation occurs after love has suffered a severe blow, this can be excruciating.

When a separation takes place, at least one of the parties has thought the matter over carefully. Separation is usually a terribly painful decision for both parties. Both the "dumper" and the "dumpee" have undoubtedly been through a mental ordeal as they have weighed the consequences with some degree of dread. Since a separation radically alters one's lifestyle, many people have mixed feelings and invariably regret some aspect of their decision. Separation is rarely as easy or pain-free as it might appear on the surface.

Under these severe circumstances, couples commonly separate and reconcile a number of times before reaching a "final resolution." Even after a final decision to divorce has been made, one or both may make efforts to reconcile. This is all part of "the ride" we are examining in this chapter.

## Moving Away from One Another

Separation occurs in stages, not in one fell swoop. In stage one, relational separation is more a *moving away from something* than it is a movement *toward* something. Think about your own separation, if that is what you are facing. More than likely you are clear about what you are moving away from. You have some idea about what has *not* worked in the relationship. But what are you moving *toward*? For most people that is much less clear.

Often, we move away from the pain only to find that we miss the "life" that existed in the relationship. At least on the surface, the painful "known" of the relationship appears a better choice than the lonely unknown. It can be easy to impulsively walk out the door in a fit of rage, vowing never again to live the way you have been living. For a while, the relief is wonderful. But you may not be prepared for the utter silence and emptiness that awaits you at your new apartment.

## Second-Guessing Ourselves

After spending some time sitting alone in the quiet, you may have second thoughts. As bad as the relationship was, you may find that from a distance, it does not seem quite so bad. You now miss many things about the relationship.

In this early phase of a separation, you can easily begin to *second-guess yourself* and your decision to leave your partner. This second stage is a time of churning emotions and unruly thoughts. You may feel a loss of confidence and wonder if you are making good decisions. The opinions of others combined with your self-doubts make for a wild ride.

Add to our unmanageable emotions those of our partners. They are just as upset, in their own particular way. While you may believe that they are "doing just fine," this is rarely the case. They are undoubtedly engaged in their own version of the second-guessing game. Even those who steadfastly assert

their certainty about the separation go through times when
they question their decision.

This self-doubt leaves you vulnerable to wavering back
and forth. Couples commonly separate and reunite many
times before finally deciding to reconcile or divorce. The
ride, however, can be grueling.

Jack Williamson and Mary Ann Salerno, in their wonderful book *Divorce: Six Ways to Get through the Bad Times*,
suggest that self-doubt is a common characteristic of stage
two. They note that this stage is characterized by questions
about whom you can trust: "A feeling of doubt warns us
that we do not have enough valid information. We need to
seek more facts, and ask more questions. The distraction
and anger caused by doubt will lead you to try to make each
aspect of the divorce a simplistic, dualistic, either/or, yes/no,
up/down, right/wrong situation. It's not. Give it up. Being
'right' might bring you a moment's satisfaction in a bloody
battle, but I implore you to go for winning the war—the war
with yourself, to regain your self-esteem and your balance.
It takes longer, but it's worth it."[1]

## Blame

During stage three of the separation, you will be tempted
to *affix blame*. In our attempts to maintain a balance during this situation, we are desperate to understand what is
happening and why. As Williamson and Salerno note, we
will want to cast blame. We will want to affix responsibility
for this mess onto someone, sometimes even ourselves. But
this narrow focus is rarely helpful or accurate. Separations
are rarely simple matters.

Our inclination to blame ourselves or others is terribly simplistic. By that I mean that in our attempt to understand, we try to reduce this complex situation to a limited number of explanations. *It is impossible and foolish to attribute the condition of your shaken world to a limited number of explanations.* This is not to say that we should avoid contemplation—but we must engage in it with an open heart.

You may feel a strong temptation, before and during a separation, to attack your spouse. None of us wants to look in the mirror and admit that we have helped create the conflict. So, as a defense against our already weakened self-esteem, we point fingers. But this can get a bit confusing. The very person we are so angry with is also the person that we loved, married, and may still want to engage in positive conversation.

Thus, we war with ourselves. We are engaged in a battle of ambivalence. Love, hate. Like, dislike. Envy, fear. Sadness, relief. The emotions are all so complex and paralyzing. "The paralysis of analysis," it has been called. It typically includes attacking the one we would so like to be close to and putting ourselves down for not having a clearer understanding and resolve about the situation. Williamson and Salerno remind us, "Blame tricks us into believing that by being upset, we can rewrite history."[2] If only it were that easy.

**Forgiveness**

In stage four of the separation process, we are ready to attempt *forgiveness.* This can be a very difficult and drawn-out process.

Holding onto our right to be angry does no good. It only ruins our life, and the other person may not even know about our agony. Spewing venom against our mate does even less good. Revisiting how you, the "righteous," have been wronged will not make you whole again. You have undoubtedly been hurt; you are entitled, even encouraged, to nurture your wounded "self." But that is different from nurturing a grudge.

The wounds from your troubled marriage may be very deep. You may have lived with your spouse for some time after learning that you were no longer loved. This had to be a grueling experience. You may have been betrayed multiple times, leading you to separate from your spouse. Perhaps your own betrayal led to a separation. Regardless, the great challenge is to decide how you want to respond to your wounds. The ability to choose how you will respond is an incredibly powerful tool. Choose wisely.

President Lincoln was asked how he would treat the rebellious Southerners when they had finally been defeated and returned to the Union of the United States. The questioner expected Lincoln to demand vengeance, but he answered, "I will treat them as if they had never been away."[3]

The book of James is replete with admonitions about how to handle some of our difficult situations and painful emotions:

> Consider it pure joy, my brothers, whenever you face trials of many kinds, because you know that the testing of your faith develops perseverance.
>
> James 1:2–3

Everyone should be quick to listen, slow to speak and slow
to become angry, for man's anger does not bring about the
righteous life that God desires.

James 1:19–20

Speak and act as those who are going to be judged by the
law that gives freedom, because judgment without mercy
will be shown to anyone who has not been merciful. Mercy
triumphs over judgment!

James 2:12–13

The book of Luke tells the story of a wealthy man who
had two sons (see Luke 15:11–32). The younger, impetuous
and unbalanced, asked his father for his share of the family fortune. The younger son left the security of family and
friends and headed out to explore the world. He squandered
his inheritance in wild living, while the responsible older
son stayed back to help manage the family estate. When the
younger son came to his senses, he realized that life back
home was not so bad. But how would his father and brother
greet him upon his return?

The story has the potential for bitterness and revenge.
Should the boy be turned away when he comes home?
Should he have to prove himself before regaining his position in the family? Should he be punished? The father of the
prodigal certainly had the right to exact payment from his
son for his rebellion. But that was not in his heart. Rather,
he called out to his son from a distance, welcoming him
home to feast together. Forgiveness is sweet, both for the
giver and receiver.

The story, of course, is a reflection of Christ's love and
forgiveness for us. Each of us has squandered the gifts of our
lives and stand in need of forgiveness. Instead of being the
harsh father we might expect, Christ stands at the banquet
table ready to celebrate our homecoming.

## Tad and Bev

Separation often includes a veritable seesaw of emotions. Tad and Bev had been married for thirteen years
and had three lovely daughters. Like a mosaic of sunlight
and shadow, their marriage seemed a picture of both good
and bad times. But painful experiences had taken their
toll, leaving Tad and Bev another statistic. Tad, reflecting
on their past, pondered whether to meet with his wife
or not. The divorce would be final in days. Why would
she want to talk at this point? He wondered if this was
another "game."

He reflected on all the times they had fought over
seemingly inconsequential issues. At the onset of their
relationship he had enjoyed her emotional temperament.
She had a zest for life that appealed to him. While he took
many things in stride, even the slightest misunderstanding seemed to be enough for an emotional reaction from
her. He was not one for fighting and, as the years wore
on, came to resent Bev's fiery temper.

In their latter years together, they challenged each other
more than they comforted one another. Still, Tad would
have been willing to hang in there. Bev, however, made the
decision to leave. It was a torturous time for him. Normally
a stoical man, Tad was brought to his emotional knees by

the separation. Requests to reconcile were rejected. She met his pleas for counseling, negotiating, even sharing a simple meal together with impassive rejection. She was steadfast in moving away from him.

A few months after leaving him, Bev had phoned to talk, much as she had done this day. She said she had experienced a change of heart and wanted him to reconsider. She was now willing to see a psychologist to get help. Reconsider he did, now to his dismay. Tad resumed his relationship with Bev only to bump into the same issues once again—resentment and ultimate rejection.

This "dance" occurred several times, always with the same result. Tad and Bev tried repeatedly to make their relationship work. They went to a few counseling sessions but gave up when the results were discouraging. Each attempt at reconciliation took its toll. Tad's heart reluctantly relinquished the desire to keep their marriage alive.

Tad was not able to focus on his job that sunny day after Bev's early morning call. He spent several hours replaying the last year in his mind. His stomach ached as he thought about her plea to talk again. Could this be the time that things could finally be worked out? Or should he "shut it down," as a good friend had advised? "How many times do you need to get burned?" his friend chastened. That question has no simple answer. The heart does not easily relinquish its desire.

**Trauma Bonding**

I have been asked on many occasions to explain why a woman or a man stays in an abusive relationship. Why, when the reasons for leaving seem obvious, do they refuse to leave? Some of the same factors evident in an abusive relationship are at play in a marriage gone awry.

When I am called into court as an "expert witness," I am often reminded that relationships are incredibly complex. I repeatedly see people stay in dysfunctional relationships. How can we explain the glue that holds conflicting partners together? Some researchers believe it is the product of *trauma bonding.*

Research on trauma bonding asserts that the mixture of intensely positive and negative experiences creates a bond that is nearly indissoluble. Something occurs in this pairing of horrible and delightful experiences that holds the couple together.

Trauma bonding may partially explain the cycle of violence, which asserts that there are predictable phases in abusive relationships: an initial tension-building phase leads to an explosive phase, which culminates in a remorseful "honeymoon" phase. Perhaps portions of this cycle fit troubled marriages as well.

We can see that most marriages are a composite of good, bad, and neutral experiences. Marriages are not all bad, in spite of the feelings one may have for their partner at a particular moment. They are also not all good, in spite of amorous feelings at certain junctures in the relationship. Rather, they are a composite of feelings that range between torment and ecstasy. Each of us must avoid the temptation to see things in absolute terms; the challenge is to see the gradations of gray that exist in all people.

## The Legal Dance

The time after hearing that you are no longer loved can be as unpredictable as the weather in Washington. It is a tenuous time—often an impending separation is on the horizon—when the slightest false move can mean the difference between reconciliation and attorneys waging a fault-finding court battle. With emotions raw from months, if not years, of conflict, it does not take much to send negotiations into a whirling downward spiral.

Ultimately, during the separation dance, the marital struggles can take on a legal dimension. The dance done under these difficult conditions is often clumsy and awkward, filled with fear and trepidation. Deep within, each partner wants an amicable separation and perhaps even hopes that reconciliation may still be possible.

Tad could feel the fragility of the situation. Bev's phone call felt like a power play to him. He doubted her sincerity in reconciling. Yet she repeatedly echoed the "right" words: She stated that she wanted the relationship to work. He did not want to push her away and certainly did not want to involve attorneys. But he also felt confused and seriously considered seeking legal counsel. He sensed little true effort on Bev's part to hang in there and do the work necessary to heal their troubled marriage.

Author Micki McWade notes the dynamics that can take a partnership of trust and respect into divorce court. Problems are created "by the couple indulging in power plays and hurling mean-spirited remarks at each other. Becoming embroiled in these scenarios takes the relationship from bad to worse. Lawyers back up their clients, so there are four people fighting, which makes for double trouble."[4] Going to court encourages competitiveness, greed, and revenge.

Consider how you are handling this time of separation. What attitude do you bring to the negotiations? Are you

- hostile and combative?
- distant and defensive?
- safe and cautious?
- friendly and giving?

What attitude is most likely to be effective at the bargaining table? What might you consider changing at this point that would create a cooperative setting?

## The Dance of Intimacy

Fortunately, even a destructive relationship often contains the seeds of possibility and can be revised into a positive experience. Couples can, at any time, stop their negative interactions and choose a more thoughtful and considerate exchange. Doing this takes a change of heart. Both must choose to end the verbal volleys and decide what they truly want to see happen. With so much at stake, honesty, as well as an understanding of your core values and purposes, is a must.

The dance of intimacy requires that you are vulnerable with your spouse in ways you may never have been before. It requires that you speak from your most tender and fragile self. With an open heart, you must share your deepest hurts and desires. Done in a conciliatory way, this kind of sharing can melt conflict and bring two people together again.

Perhaps you recognize yourself in some of the examples used in this chapter. Perhaps you have been embroiled in a heated battle with your spouse and felt that you were unable to extricate yourself from the turmoil. Maybe the roller coaster ride made it impossible for you to relinquish your bitterness. You can move away from the emotional speed bumps. You can advance beyond your current win/lose mentality to a cooperative relationship. You can "give in" and win.

## Ending the Ride

Tad and Bev were similar to many couples with whom I have worked. They continued to engage in emotional free-for-alls. Their conflict never seemed to lead to resolution and ultimately eroded their affection for one another.

Noted marriage authority Dr. John Gottman, author of *The Seven Principles for Making Marriage Work*, says that unresolved conflict, as well as unforgiveness, is a key element leading to the erosion of love. He emphasizes that couples must learn techniques to manage their conflict. He suggests that there are "four horsemen" in predicting divorce:

- criticism
- contempt
- defensiveness
- stonewalling[5]

These components, almost always present in relationships that dissolve, are also evident with couples who continue their destructive dances. The "four horsemen" will almost always create a lack of intimacy, an erosion of love, and separation or divorce.

If you genuinely want reconciliation with your spouse, you *must* manage the four horsemen. Let's look at the list more closely.

Consider *letting go of criticism*. Finding fault in your partner is easy. You can clearly see what they have done wrong and why they should be judged. Seeing your part in the entire matter is harder. Let criticism go!

Consider *letting go of contempt*. Contempt or resentment has been likened to resending bitterness back to your partner again and again. It is rehearsing all the bad things they have done. It is a terrible place to live; move on.

Consider *giving up defensiveness*. Create a spirit of openness toward your spouse. Be open to the possibility that they are changing, and be open to the possibility that you need to change as well.

Finally, consider *giving up stonewalling*. Learn to build bridges to your mate instead of barriers. Find issues you agree upon. Even if you end up separating or divorcing, chances are you will be in some kind of ongoing relationship with them. Create a relationship of harmony.

Even after a separation, when love may be in short supply, goodwill can be fostered and in some cases bring about reconciliation. Wanting the best for your spouse, especially when you are hurting, can be a powerful antidote for a damaged relationship.

## Summary

Many people hold the tremendous misconception that marital negotiations proceed along a straight, linear path. Many believe that the path from love lost to divorce court is a direct path. Nothing could be further from the truth. The path is often a complex and painful labyrinth. One can easily get lost in it.

What do you need to avoid getting lost? As you reflect on this chapter, remember to keep a support network close at hand. Remain actively prayerful. Not only do you need the godly wisdom that comes through meditation and prayer, but you also need the peace that comes from spending quiet time with God. Seek professional Christian counseling. This is not a time to do it on your own, and a caring professional will help you navigate the hoops and hurdles that follow the breakdown of a loving marriage. Finally, keep an open heart. Anything can, and very well may, happen. In spite of the speed bumps on the path, try to keep your heart and mind open to what can develop in your relationship with your spouse. Be cautious about negative forecasting or premature foreclosing of possibilities. Keep a clear head and a generous heart, and you will know the right thing to do at the right time.

# 6

~~~~~~~~~~~~~~~~~~~~~~~~~~~~~~~~~~~~~~~~~~

# FRIENDSHIP IN TIMES
## OF NEED

*Each friend represents a world in us, a
world not born until they arrive, and
it is only by meeting that a new world
is born.*

Anaïs Nin

Jessica laid the phone down and sat silently. She was too
numb to cry, too frightened to scream, too confused to
understand her own thoughts.

Her husband, Darren, a sales representative with a major
plumbing firm, spent nearly two out of every four weeks

on the road. This trip had taken him to Atlanta. He had just made his routine evening call. Sadly, there was nothing routine about this call. She could tell by the hesitancy in his voice that something was wrong.

"Jessica," he began slowly. "I've come to a decision. You know that I've been struggling with my feelings toward you. I've tried to bring back the old emotions, but they just aren't there. I've made a decision, and I don't want to fight about it. When I get home I want to move out for a while. I'm not saying it's over, but I want you to prepare for the worst."

For the moment, Jessica decided not to protest his decision. Her hand shook as she placed the receiver back in its cradle. She and Darren had talked about their marital problems many times. She had tried repeatedly to dissuade Darren from taking any drastic actions as she coped with the waning warmth in their marriage. But it was no use; his heart wasn't in it. He gave only a half-hearted effort to address their differences and refused counseling. She now felt resigned to a separation.

When she'd stopped shaking, she reached for the phone to call a friend in whom she could confide. Thankfully, she had spent years cultivating a strong network of friends who gathered in both good times and bad. Tonight she would sit in her favorite rocking chair and tearfully share her sorrow with her best friend. Life had never looked so bleak.

Jessica had seen the separation coming. Despite the warning signs, when the news hit she could hardly breathe, let alone think straight. She needed support, and she needed it immediately.

During a crisis like this, the flood of emotions that overwhelm us makes it hard to think clearly. A few objective friends can offer clear-headed opinions. Jessica's friends offered her comfort, compassion, and direction when she was hardly able to care for her basic needs.

"Without my friends," Jessica said, "I would not have been able to make it. They gave me a place to stay while I figured out what I wanted to do next. They made meals for my daughters and me and even offered to drive me to some of my appointments. I couldn't work for a few days, so they let me crash at their place while I considered my options. Most importantly, they helped me to think at a time when I was very confused. They have been great."

## The Importance of Friends

What was it about the hit show *Cheers* that captured Americans' hearts? Certainly each character had something inviting to offer. We could smile as we saw some part of ourselves in Norm's unwillingness to take responsibility or Cliff's inability to accept reality. But more importantly, I am convinced, we loved the sense of community in a place where "everybody knows your name." Imagine walking in the door and having everyone look up and greet you by name!

More recently, the show *Friends* has reminded us of the importance of being intimately connected to people who understand how life is for us. They help us through the tough times and celebrate our victories with us.

Dr. Thomas Whiteman and Randy Petersen, co-authors of *Starting Over,* remind us of the importance of friendships. They assert that friendships are part of an intricate web of needs that were evident in us from the foundation of the world. God created us with a need for security and significance. To illustrate this, the authors cite the smash television hit *Survivor,* where players form alliances in order to avoid getting voted off the island. Whiteman and Petersen write, "Alliances make us strong, whether they're international treaties, political maneuvering, TV-show finagling, or marriages. Partners protect each other. Families provide for their members' physical needs."[1]

The importance of having friends to provide emotional support cannot be overstated. A network of friends can make the difference between coping effectively and suffering mercilessly during a separation. Friends can help you cope, although they can also hinder your growth if you do not choose them wisely.

Take a moment and conduct a mental review of your friendships. Whom are you truly connected to? Whom could you call on a moment's notice for emotional support?

### How Important Are Friends?

Your life has changed dramatically. Not only have you lost the security of your primary relationship, but also your routine has been completely disrupted. You will require extra help in maintaining a sense of equilibrium. Friends are critical to your well-being at this time for several reasons:

First, *friends offer us a place to vent all the feelings that come with a broken relationship.* Flooded with emotion, you need a safe place where you can vent. In the comfortable living room of a friend, you can let your hair down and allow the tears to flow. This grief process is a critical part of your healing, and safe friends are an essential part of the process.

After her sudden separation, Jessica had a vast array of feelings that she was not prepared to handle. She was surprised at how frightened she felt and how unsure she was of her future. Suddenly she did not know what to do with her time or how to manage her anger and fear. Her friends helped to settle her down.

Second, *friends offer another perspective on your situation.* You know the saying, "I can't see the forest for the trees"? Friends help you acknowledge and visualize the forest. They offer you a broader perspective so you don't get mired down in the details of your crisis.

When in the middle of a crisis, you will have a tendency to see only one or two sides of a problem. You will naturally roll the same thoughts over in your mind because you lack the flexibility to consider the problem from alternate positions. Jessica, thankfully, had good friends who were invaluable in helping her look at things from another angle. They reminded her of things she had said and things she had forgotten that could impact her current perspective.

Third, *a good friend knows how to tell us things that we may not want to hear in a way that doesn't devastate us.* We all have defense mechanisms. Most of us want to know the truth but feel some level of fragility about hearing it. Good friends find that delicate balance between slamming us with the truth and letting us languish in our myopic opinions. They support us and confront us. They offer us information upon request. Good friends have no need to pontificate upon their truths and opinions.

Jessica wanted her friends to offer their opinions, but she wanted those opinions to be delivered in a gentle and thoughtful manner. She was feeling very raw and didn't want to be confronted in a way that would only make her feel worse about her situation. She needed truth in small doses, and her friends knew how to offer that. They spoke to her calmly but honestly, reassuring her that they cared for her no matter what decisions she made.

Fourth, *good friends offer wisdom.* This wisdom is not just good advice but a deeper level of insight. Wise friends have a knack for putting things in their proper, godly perspective. Wisdom is said to have three components: love, firmness, and knowledge.[2] Look for these traits in those from whom you seek and accept guidance.

Jessica's friends came from different backgrounds, but several attended her church. They shared similar values and gave her advice sparingly, with an understanding of scriptural principles. She was able to trust that what they told her would not violate the values she held dearly.

Fifth, *friends help us maintain a sense of community.* Already feeling fragmented from a broken relationship and possible separation, we look to friends to provide a critical sense of grounding. They offer acceptance and a sense of continuity in our life. Because broken marriages cause strife in some friendships, you may find it necessary to turn to other friends or even to make new friends. Still, your friends will be very important.

Jessica still needed to go on with her life in spite of her husband's decision. She had children who needed to get to school and needed help with their homework. She also had a church to which she still wanted to belong. Her friends could help her maintain some of the routines in her life, and that return to normalcy would help in her recovery.

Finally, *friends give acceptance.* At a time when your self-esteem may be challenged, friends still care about you. At a time when you may feel rejected and rejectable, friends offer affirmation. They have seen us at our best and worst and still manage to like us.

Jessica's girlfriends had known her for several years. They knew one another's foibles and could accept one another and even tease each other for their humanity. They felt no need to judge one another since each had revealed their own weaknesses to the other.

I hope you have a reservoir of folks with whom you have cultivated relationships over the years and whom you can now lean on. Reach out to others and let them know that you need some extra TLC at this difficult time. Whether the possibilities come through your church involvement, community activities, or other outlets, reach out. Never take your friendships for granted.

## Friendships Gone Awry

When relationships crack and possibly crumble, no matter how things eventually turn out, the trauma will place pressure upon your friendships. Those friendships will face unique challenges and perhaps new demands. Let's look at a few of them.

### Absence of Friendships

The first possible serious problem concerning friendships is actually one that occurred before the turmoil of lost love: Unfortunately, you may find yourself without friends during this crisis. You want to reach out to others, but you find your address book painfully empty.

You may not have noticed this situation before. Why would you? Perhaps you leaned on your spouse for emotional and social support more than you realized. You bumped into friendly people at church, work, and other areas of interest, but they were friendly, not friends. Now you may realize that you have more acquaintances than true friends. You felt that you were being supported adequately, but when the crisis came and you were ready to reach out, no one was there to take your hand.

Don't be surprised if this situation describes you. Many people have made a number of acquaintances, but when it comes time to pick up the phone and talk about very personal matters, they freeze. They have no one they feel comfortable calling to pour out the crushing details of their life.

If you find yourself in this situation, you have a challenge ahead of you. Not only must you face the difficulties of lost love and all the decisions that come with it, but you also must face the dilemma of developing a network of support. Never fear, because this task is doable, and now is an excellent opportunity to do it. *It needed to be done anyway!* Take this opportunity to reach out.

But how, you may ask, can you build a support network where none exists? It is not easy, so you will need to review your lifestyle and your likes and dislikes and *get involved.* Consider the possibilities:

- Become active in a Sunday school class.
- Sing in a choir.
- Volunteer for the Red Cross.
- Join the Rotary or another service organization.
- Become active in a local club.
- Join a support group.
- Take a part-time job where you will meet people.

The list of possibilities is endless, but they will all take work to develop. The results will not be immediate because you are planting seeds and waiting for them to grow. The sooner you start, the faster the results.

Let me add one final word of caution: *Do not even think about going this alone.* Though you may be isolated and feel that no one cares about you, don't get stuck in this mindset. Others are ready to care about you if you will give them the chance.

### Shattered Friendships

Tragically, lost love and possible marital separation can also lead to problems in other relationships. For most of us, marriage is the context in which we nurture and maintain other friendships. Many times couples are friends with other couples they have met through work, church, or neighborhood proximity. When a marital relationship is disrupted, even temporarily, it can play havoc in those other friendships.

Brent and Susan had been married for eight years when an affair by Brent led to a temporary separation. Understandably, Susan was devastated to learn of his office liaison. Although the discovery promptly led Brent to discontinue the relationship, its end did not deter Susan from wanting some space to think things over.

> *Two are better than one, because they have a good return for their work: If one falls down, his friend can help him up. But pity the man who falls and has no one to help him up! Also, if two lie down together, they will keep warm. But how can one keep warm alone? Though one may be overpowered, two can defend themselves. A cord of three strands is not quickly broken.*
>
> Ecclesiastes 4:9–12

Brent had maintained the secret relationship for several months, leading a double life with neighbors, co-workers, and church couples with whom they were friends. Obviously, the discovery and breakup of the office affair created challenges at work. Brent and Susan had many decisions to face, and the ripple effect on their friendships was enormous.

Susan wanted to tell her friends, who were also friends of Brent. While he did not relish having this news cast about in their social circle, he understood her need to confide in others. Susan did not want Brent to work in the same office with the "other woman." Thus Brent was forced to change jobs. Friendships at the office were shattered, and he was suddenly without a support network that he had previously taken for granted.

The ripple effect of their separation did not stop there. News of their separation spread quickly through their church. While some refused to take sides, others quickly judged Brent to be the "bad guy," and he felt the strain in their shared friendships. Some church members were furious with him and encouraged Susan to file for a divorce.

Susan, too, felt the strain on her friendships. She said, "It was amazing to me to hear and feel the reactions of our friends. Everyone had an opinion. I couldn't believe how quickly people jumped in to tell me what to do. I heard everything from 'You need to forgive and forget about it' to 'You need to leave him and get on with your life.' It was terribly confusing. It really shook up some of my friendships. All I wanted was a listening ear and some sound counsel, and I feel like I got everything but that. After a while all I wanted was to be left alone."

Susan had a very difficult struggle in the months following their separation. She lost some friends when she refused to follow their rigid advice. She became embittered with some for their harsh stance toward Brent. Fortunately, she came to appreciate a few of her more understanding friends even more as they were able to come alongside her with love, support, and gentle counsel.

### Splintered Friendships

While sometimes relationships are shattered, they are more often splintered. By that I mean that friendships are challenged and strained, and the relationship is weakened, although not broken.

Consider again the volatile emotions you experience when your marriage feels vulnerable and your security is threatened. Bringing others' opinions and feelings into the mix creates conditions ripe for additional conflict. While you are longing for acceptance and support, friends often are not clear about what role they are to play. Are they supposed to side with you when you vent your deeply-held feelings about your partner? Are they supposed to spur you into action? Should they simply listen? Many find it difficult to know how to behave when a friend goes through this kind of struggle.

> *Your healing can be helped or hurt by the company you keep.*
>
> Thomas Whiteman
> and Randy Petersen,
> *Starting Over*

Emotional challenges in marriage often lead to other changes. When a couple separates, it brings a literal move as well. Sometimes it is a move across town; sometimes it is a move across the state. The effect of the move on the friendship cannot be overstated. Trying to maintain the support you need while also looking for a new job and a new apartment, caring for children, and taking care of other tasks can be overwhelming. Friendships can become splintered simply by the logistics of the whole situation.

Bringing the feelings of families into the mix can create another quagmire of challenges. While we would all like to believe that families, including parents, will offer support while maintaining objectivity, this is a tall order. Typically, families are ready to rally behind their own. Unfortunately, choosing sides will only aggravate an already tenuous situation. Both partners need support and affirmation, but they do not need anyone to take up an offense against their partner. Because a separation is, by definition, a temporary situation, every caution must be taken not to stir up emotions in your family against your spouse. It will only hurt things later on if the relationship can be restored.

## Enmeshed Friendships

As Brent and Susan found out, everyone seems to have a ready opinion as to how to run your life. When a tragedy hits, folks seem willing to offer their point of view, often with a certainty that they have the answers for all your problems. While this may be a bit over-dramatized, it is true all too frequently. Why is this kind of enmeshment—another attempt to control your life—such a common and fatal phenomenon?

First, enmeshment seems to be so common because many people receive secondary gains from others' problems. Sadly, too many troubled folks get some kind of charge out of other people's problems. They are "drama junkies," and the closer to home that drama occurs, the better. While we would hope that they want the drama to end and reconciliation and hope to prevail, they may, sadly, have a need for the struggle to remain.

Another reason is the apparent plethora of armchair psychologists out there. Having read the latest, greatest self-help book on the topic, they are ready to offer their version of the gospel according to them. While they may be sincere, they may have a lack of boundaries about when and how to offer help. Beware of the "expert" who

- offers their opinion without request
- tells you there is one way of doing things
- gives you their opinion in a judgmental manner
- makes you feel guilty or ashamed of what you are doing

Perhaps the best thing a good friend can do in a precarious situation is listen, offer hope, and agree to earnestly pray for both parties. Becoming enmeshed only compromises a friend's ability to be helpful.

### Controlling Friendships

A stronger version of the enmeshed relationship is the controlling friendship. In this case a friend goes beyond enmeshment and, for whatever reason, uses the opportunity to control you. You end up enduring the challenges of a separation while also trying to make sense out of the control issues of a friend. Controlling friends will spout off their opinions about

- how you should feel about your spouse
- how you should behave toward your spouse
- what you should do about your living situation
- how often you should be seeing your spouse
- how often you should be seeing your friends

Controlling friends have some heavy needs that are being met as a result of your crisis. They have undoubtedly made a practice of focusing on others' problems while possibly neglecting their own lives. While they certainly display kindness, it is with questionable motives. They need *your* friendship!

These kinds of friends do not really know how to be a friend. They have a twisted notion of what friendship really means. They have porous boundaries and cannot separate what they need from what you need.

- You need a listening ear. They talk and give advice.
- You need appropriate, limited affection. They smother you with affection.
- You need understanding. They offer their rendition of what is taking place.
- You need someone to empathize with your feelings. They tell you about their struggles.
- You need someone to not show partiality. They become the judge and jury of your spouse.
- You need someone to let you make mistakes. They tell you exactly what to do and how to do it.
- You need freedom to be you. They shame you into believing you must think and act their way.

Steer clear of those who try to control you in these ways. This is not the kind of friendship you need.

## Healthy Friendships during Lost Love

With so many pitfalls to friendships, do you have any hope for developing and maintaining healthy relationships? Can this crisis, in fact, be an opportunity for strengthening and deepening a friendship? Absolutely. But it may take some work as well as energy, which may be in short supply right now.

Take a step back and consider how friendships are working for you. Consider what can be gained by altering some friendships, adding friendships, and perhaps even letting go of some friends. What are the opportunities facing you at this time in your life?

### A Time to Strengthen Friendships

Now that I have shared the bad news, let's lighten up with some good news. This crisis can be a time when you learn about true friendship. You will learn who can be counted upon and trusted. You will undoubtedly spend many hours leaning upon others and telling them your deepest secrets. It can be a tremendous time of healing and bonding.

> *The scripture was fulfilled that says, "Abraham believed God, and it was credited to him as righteousness," and he was called God's friend.*
>
> James 2:23

I have had the joy of watching many separated people spend quality time with friends and develop relationships that will endure for a lifetime. I have known the delight of spending time in prayer with friends during a crisis and feeling the cords of friendship grow stronger. I hope you have had that experience in your life as well. This is your chance to have it again.

However, experiencing the hope that comes through friendship will require that you reach outside yourself, perhaps outside your comfort zone, and trust others with your burdens. We are admonished in Scripture to "carry each other's burdens, and in this way you will fulfill the law of Christ" (Gal. 6:2).

If you choose your friends wisely, share information appropriately, and seek counsel in a timely manner, your circle of friends and support will sustain you through this trial. In turn, you will learn how to be a better friend when others need you in the future.

### Friendship with God

Perhaps the most important thing that can happen in a person's life during a crisis is that they learn to lean on the everlasting arms of the Lord. Yes, this can sound trite and simplistic. But is it possible that you could learn to lean into the Word of God and by doing so learn more about this friend at this challenging time of your life? Consider the promises inherent in friendship with God.

First, *God is knowable.* What a wonderful thing! We can learn all about him through his Son, Jesus. We can learn about his ways and his desires for our life. Through creation, the Word, and Christ, God can be known personally. "Now this is eternal life: that they may know you, the only true God, and Jesus Christ, whom you have sent" (John 17:3).

Second, *he wants to be friends with us.* He longs to have a relationship with us, his children. He calls us "dear friends" (see 1 John 2:7). He waits for us to call upon him in our time of distress (see John 15:14–17).

Third, *he offers us magnificent gifts:* eternal life and peace everlasting. "Peace I leave with you; my peace I give you. I do not give to you as the world gives. Do not let your hearts be troubled and do not be afraid" (John 14:27).

Fourth, *our Lord has endured all the struggles that we face and more.* He can identify with us in our sufferings (see Rom. 8:31–32). This is the kind of friend we need in the middle of the battle.

## Summary

We have seen that friendship can help us meet the challenges of lost love or separation. When we experience stress it usually affects many parts of our lives, including friendships. But by the same token, friendships can be one thing which God uses to offer us a port in the storm.

Friendships can be a tremendous blessing or a horrendous heartache. This chapter has offered you a few pointers on how to set clear, healthy boundaries so that your friendships will be beneficial to your healing, not hurtful to you.

Finally, we must remind ourselves that while some friendships may fail us, we have an open invitation to discover a perfect friendship with Jesus Christ. Lean into the Word of God and find comfort in the words of the psalmist when he says, "But you are a shield around me, O LORD; you bestow glory on me and lift up my head" (Ps. 3:3).

# 7

## FAMILY MATTERS

*Every love we feel—our love for our
partners, our children, our friends,
and our community—comes with its
own set of complications.*

Alexandra Stoddard

When Trisha looked at her in-laws, a wave of panic began to build in her stomach. She wondered and worried about what they must be thinking about her. She had known them for most of her adult life; they were family to her. But at this family gathering, much had clearly changed.

This birthday gathering was supposed to be a time of celebration for her son. But Trisha was far too tense to enjoy herself. She knew that Rob's parents were aware of the problems she and Rob were having. She knew they were thinking, "How could you think about leaving our son after eighteen years of marriage?"

They exchanged greetings and small talk, avoiding the obvious bigger issues. Trisha felt more uncomfortable than she had ever imagined. She dared not bring up her real feelings. How could she tell them that the reason she and Rob were having problems was because Rob had been having an affair with another woman? Though that relationship was apparently over, her trust in him had been shattered. She hoped that her anger and deep hurt could be contained during the party.

Trisha wondered why she had agreed to meet with her husband in his parents' home. Now that she and Rob were separated, even being in the same room with them was painful. Yet she could hardly refuse to be a part of her son's birthday party.

Trisha sat by herself for a moment and reflected on the drastic changes that were now happening to this portion of her family. The bonds had been broken, and everyone in the family was undoubtedly feeling it.

"How do people handle these kinds of things?" Trisha asked me during a counseling session. "How am I supposed to pretend that I'm happy to be with my husband and his family for these family celebrations when what I really want is distance? I feel like a balloon ready to burst. And I certainly don't feel like getting together to celebrate."

"This is a part of the separation you were not prepared for," I said. "Maybe you had imagined that you would just be separating from your husband and hadn't anticipated all of these loose ends. Seeing your husband and his family brought up lots of pain, probably because it made you remember better times with them before the separation."

"I could never have predicted there would be so many issues to work through. Do we still get together for Christmas? Do we still attend the same church as before? Do I have him over for his birthday in a few weeks? What are the rules for these kinds of things?"

"Part of the problem is that there are very few rules about how to handle these sorts of issues," I told her. "They are bound to be thorny, and you will need to listen carefully to your heart, talk to your husband, and work out the details. I do suspect that after you have worked your way through a few of these situations, they will get easier."

"Yes, I think you are right," she said. "But that doesn't make it any easier today, that's for sure. I hate this stuff. I hate having to think about the other woman. I hate seeing Rob. I hate not seeing Rob. I hate Rob telling me that he doesn't know if he loves me anymore. I hate seeing his family, and I miss them at the same time. Being aware of what is happening doesn't make all the bad feelings go away."

"No, I don't suppose it does," I said. "This is another loss for you, and you are going to have to accept it. You are not one big, happy family anymore."

## Marriage and the Family

Families embody our hopes, fears, and expectations. We expect a lot from them, often more than they can possibly deliver.

Lost love, or even a discussion of marital separation, plays havoc with the routines, hopes, and comforts of the family. The ripple effects of lost love move quickly through the extended family like a spark in a tinder-dry forest.

We need to remember that when we married, we married an entire family. Remember that an entire family, along with our friends, gathered to celebrate the beginning of the marriage. The family had a vested interest in the stability and integrity of the union. The extended family has hopes and expectations of us, and we feel them strongly.

When Trisha first met Rob's family, she was very nervous. She wanted to make a good impression. Thankfully, they were easy to get to know. They welcomed her and made her feel accepted and loved. She came from a small family, with just one younger sister. But Rob had two sisters and a brother, and immediately Trisha felt like she was a part of something. Rob's siblings and his parents lived in the same town that she and Rob lived in, so everybody usually got together once or twice a week for gin rummy parties, videos, birthday celebrations, or even just spontaneous gatherings to eat pizza and visit. It was all a lot of fun. They were a close family, and she was happy to be part of it.

She was also aware that the feelings were mutual. The family enjoyed her and seemed to appreciate the qualities she brought to the group. She had a knack for joining right in with the zaniness that inevitably occurred when they all got together. Even in the midst of family crises, they had a high level of solidarity.

Can you remember when you first visited "the family"? Were you a little nervous? Perhaps you simply met your spouse's parents and were gradually introduced to the entire gang. Did you go over for dinner and sit around trying to act natural and collected? Did you wear your Sunday best, or did you decide to let them see you in your blue jeans? Whatever you decided, it probably became clear that you were getting involved in a relationship with a larger family unit.

## Ripples in the Family

Trisha had caught Rob having an affair several years earlier, and they had attended counseling to mend things. Things seemed to improve for a while, but now he had done it again. Worse than that, he had tried to explain his actions by telling her that he was not sure if he still loved her. That was the final blow for her, and she made it clear to him that she and the children would need to move out.

Word spread quickly that Trisha had walked out on Rob. She had been careful not to broadcast the details leading up to her leaving, but she knew that by now people were speculating on what had happened.

While you may try to keep the lid on things, before long the family, as well as the entire community in many cases, begins to make assumptions about what is happening. Of course, they don't *know* what is going on, but they will concoct a variety of stories to explain the situation. The rumor mill will be up and running at full speed in no time.

Rob was approached by some old friends who said they'd heard he had been arrested for drunk driving. He was angry with Trisha because he assumed that she had made up the story. She assured him that she had not made up any stories about him being arrested. In fact, she hadn't told anyone other than her best friend why she had left. She did tell him that family members had heard that she had left because she was seeing another man and wanted to know if it was true. Both agreed that they would need to be extremely cautious with whom they shared intimate information about their marriage.

Both Rob and Trisha were also left wondering about what to tell family. Who could be trusted with the information? If they told one person, would it circulate around to the rest of the family? They feared the rumor mill would continue at full speed if they told no one. Yet as long as there might be a glimmer of hope for their relationship, they did not want to share too much. They were confused as to the best course of action.

## Fear of Others' Reactions

Let's listen to Trisha share how she felt about telling her family.

"After I left Rob I felt really embarrassed and didn't want anyone to know. But I talk to my mom and dad all the time, and after a week or so I felt like they had the right to know. But it was still incredibly hard to make the phone call. Even though I know they love me, I felt ashamed that something like this had happened to us. Everyone thought Rob and I were the perfect couple, and I hated disappointing my parents. And I sure didn't want to tell them all the details of what led up to my leaving. What would they think of Rob? I didn't want them to hate him.

"Before I called them I wondered how they would react. I wondered if they would judge me. I wondered if they would ask a lot of questions about what had happened. Would they ask if Rob had been unfaithful again? Would they expect me to stand by him no matter what he had done? I was a mess. I really wanted their support, but I also feared them being critical. On top of that, I was unsure about how I wanted them to react toward Rob. At times I wanted them not to take sides, and at other times I wanted them to take care of me and come to my defense. It was really confusing.

"As far as my sister went, I didn't really want her involved for a while. I usually trust her, but this felt different. She is usually able to be objective, but she can also be critical. I felt so raw and vulnerable. I couldn't handle her asking me a lot of questions. I feared that the first thing she would say was 'Did he do it to you again?' If she knew the whole story, she would be furious at Rob and might even make a snide comment about me staying in a situation that I should have left years ago. If I told her I still had feelings for Rob, she would be upset with me. I felt like a teenage girl again with my family, with all the doubts and fears of their reactions."

**The Lines Are Drawn**

Families have their own loyalties. The cliché that "blood is thicker than water" finds its meaning within the boundaries of the family. We should not be surprised to find Trisha was protected by her parents while Rob found safety and understanding in his family. Parents and siblings usually feel the tug to support a blood relative over the spouse. Lines will inevitably be drawn, compounding the pain of separation and loss.

Trisha could feel those lines at the birthday party. She felt tension between herself and her mother-in-law. While her in-laws were friendly, she felt a formality that she had never before experienced. She wanted to talk to them about the separation, but could not do so now without blaming Rob. She had seen them have a fierce loyalty to him in the past, in spite of his actions. And besides, she and Rob had agreed to try to keep the families out of their personal business as much as possible.

Perhaps you have experienced some of what Rob and Trisha went through. So many questions arise, many of which you had probably never anticipated. For example, if your spouse leaves to go to her parents' home for a respite, do you call? And if you call, what do you say? You want information, but that encroaches on the boundaries your spouse has erected to gain some space for reflection. If you don't call, do you risk giving the impression that you don't care?

Perhaps you have experienced a different reaction. You may have reached out to your family for support only to have a parent say, "You have made your bed, now lie in it." Or perhaps, "We really don't want to get caught in the middle of your struggles. We suggest that you go home and try to work it out." In this case, the lines drawn within your own family can feel even more troubling than those drawn between yourself and your in-laws. Already feeling abandoned by your spouse, feeling rejected by your family will only intensify your pain.

Any position the family takes can be precarious. Sadly, if families get embroiled in the marital separation, an adversarial quality can be ignited. Parents may side with their own child and begin to harbor negative feelings toward the son- or daughter-in-law without knowing the complete truth of what is happening. When this happens, feelings inevitably get hurt and long-term relationships may be forever strained.

### Triangulation

One of the unfortunate by-products of extended family struggles is *triangulation,* which involves getting other people embroiled in a conflict that does not truly involve them. It is the type of behavior that says, "Let's you and I talk about them." Triangulation encourages someone to take the offensive against another party, even when it is not their issue.

This is easy to do with family. In the case of Trisha and Rob, he had already gone to his parents and siblings and shared a little about what had happened in his marriage. As is often the case, he put his own spin on things. While he admitted to seeing someone else, he framed this event as a brief relationship which happened because intimacy had been missing in his marriage for some time. While not trying to make Trisha look bad, he certainly wanted to justify his actions. In the process he minimized his own responsibility for their problems and maximized her responsibilities.

The obvious danger of triangulation is that it pits one party, or family, against another person. It creates a win-lose scenario rather than keeping points of view open to create a positive outcome. In this case, Rob's parents sided with Rob. They failed to hold him fully responsible for his actions and developed some resentment toward Trisha that would stay with them for a long time. Becoming embroiled in their son's marriage difficulties would jeopardize their ability to love and accept her in the future, should the marriage survive this crisis. Even if it did not, they would still expect to be active in their grandchildren's lives.

Trisha found out soon enough about her in-laws' position. Sensing their point of view was not hard to do and created growing resentment toward them on her part.

Though Trisha and Rob had agreed not to over-involve parents or family in their struggles, this is often very difficult to do. Everyone is looking for support, and family is often the first place to turn when things are going wrong. However, because there is so much at stake, care must be taken not to over-involve the family in the strife. This separation may be short-lived, and you do not want long-term repercussions. Heated emotions shared with parents at one stage in the process are not easily changed when the struggle ends.

A few simple guidelines can help you decide how much to share with parents and family:

1. Don't share information for the purpose of attacking your spouse.
2. Don't try to get your family to side with you against your spouse.

3. Share with the intention of sharing your feelings and getting emotional support.
4. Be honest in your sharing, portraying a balanced perspective.
5. Share information cautiously with people who are capable of keeping the information confidential.

**Necessary Losses**

Honoring your losses is a major theme of this book. The enormity of lost love and possible separation cannot be talked about honestly without talking about loss. Not only has your immediate family been hurt, but part of your extended family feels vulnerable to the loss of love as well. Life feels raw and fragile for everyone involved.

So much of life is wrapped up in family affairs. Most of what is familiar in our lives, including rituals and patterns of living, involves family. Holidays are spent frantically traveling from one set of relatives to another. Many times the extended family is part of birthday parties, soccer games, and even remodeling projects. You complain about the chaos at the time, but when the gang suddenly is missing because of a separation, the magnitude of the loss is almost overwhelming. Perhaps you took for granted how important these people were to you.

Have you faced your first holiday without the extended family? If so, you have faced decisions about whether or not to try to celebrate with your spouse and his or her family. These decisions are difficult at best and excruciating at worst. Trisha chose to be with her husband and his family, but not without a great deal of consideration. Many choose to simply be alone or with close friends rather than face the barrage of questions at family gatherings.

The Scriptures were right when they said that in marriage the two shall become one flesh (Gen. 2:24). But it's more than the union of two individuals. Families marry families. Scripture gives many warnings, especially in the Old Testament, about whom to marry. God knew that marriage causes a binding not of just two people but of families.

One example of families becoming involved with one another is the story of Ruth and Naomi, found in the book of Ruth. These women from radically different cultures are brought together as daughter-in-law and mother-in-law. Both husbands die, and the wives are left alone. Ruth and her mother-in-law are thrust together to fend for themselves in hostile territory. These women from two disparate worlds are forced to rely upon one another and, of course, upon God. Ruth gives due allegiance to Naomi's wisdom and instruction as Naomi plots and follows the Lord's guidance to find a husband and protector for Ruth. With only one another to lean upon, they forge forward, finding strength in their friendship, resolve, and faith. They experience a series of disasters, yet things do work out—but not before Ruth and Naomi endure scorn, ridicule, and adversity and discover the mettle they have within.

The lesson for us in this incredible story is that of loyalty in the face of adversity. We realize who we can count on when facing trials in our lives. We often turn to the family when in desperate circumstances. Sharing the rudiments of dedication to family, Ruth says to Naomi, "Where you go I will go, and where you stay I will stay. Your people will be my people and your God my God. . . . May the LORD deal with me, be it ever so severely, if anything but death separates you and me" (Ruth 1:16–17).

The story of Ruth and Naomi is not all that different from what happens in many families today. Different cultures find one another through the bridge of love. People of different colors choose marriage in spite of cultural conflicts. Couples come together with commonalities enough to span many years. Life, with all its quirkiness, brings families together for better or worse. Lost love separates them.

Like Ruth and Naomi, you have also become one with your spouse and his or her family in so many ways. Family acceptance, involvement, and rituals of celebration are some of the ways that the two have become one flesh. Perhaps over the years you have grown close to your mother- or father-in-law. In fact, many people feel closer to their in-laws than to their own siblings or parents. This is not surprising in light of how much time you may have spent with them. Perhaps you have had the good fortune of living in close proximity to them and having them be an integral part of your daily life. Perhaps they have been active in the social lives of your children. Yet when you lose the love of your mate, you often lose the love and support of your in-laws as well.

### Keeping the Boundaries Clear and Healthy

During this time of uncertainty, one of your most beneficial tools for coping is that of setting healthy boundaries. Families are often the place where we practice setting healthy boundaries, partly because family settings are often the place where the most emotions surface, creating both tension and positive feelings.

What do I mean by healthy boundaries? Boundaries define who we want to see, how much of our lives we want to share, where we want to live, and so on. Our boundaries establish who we are. They let our families know that we are individuals, similar to them in some ways, different in others.

Trisha and Rob faced a great challenge. With emotions running high, each was tempted to vilify the other. They could have easily embroiled their children in their struggles. Thankfully, they did not do that. They worked hard to set healthy boundaries.

Both Trisha and Rob had to consider their boundaries and how they wanted to interact with their families. They carefully decided together how they would involve their family in their separation. They decided that they owed their family some explanation of what was happening, and they wanted support from them. They decided that they did not really want their families to take sides. They did not want to alienate one partner from the other's family. Because of their thoughtfulness, things worked out better for them and their family than they would have without an agreed-upon plan of action.

Unfortunately, many times we let others dictate the conditions of our social life, living arrangements, work, and so on. Or perhaps we make decisions by default. We let others talk us into things that are not good for us. When it comes to family functioning, this is a time to consider how you want to live. Some of your considerations include:

- Do I want to go back with my spouse?
- What changes would I like to see in our relationship?

- When would I want to reconcile, if that is an option?
- Do I want to tell my parents what is happening?
- Do I want my in-laws to know what is happening?
- What friends can I trust with the details of my life?
- What should we tell our children?
- How can we be most helpful to our children at this time?

## Creating a New and Better Family

If you have not had the kind of relationship with your extended family that you would have liked prior to this crisis, this can be a time to renegotiate a healthier family system. How can that be done? Here are a few pointers:

First, *decide what kind of extended family you want.* What role do you want your family to play in this crisis? Spend some time getting clear, within yourself, about what a healthy family would look like. Jot down a few notes about it.

Two, *decide whether your family can realistically meet your needs.* Some families can listen to you and are willing to be there for you. Some have healthy boundaries, knowing what is their business and what is not. Other families do not have the emotional capacity to be an anchor for you. They may be unavailable because of location, addiction issues, long-term dysfunctionality, or emotional distance and lack of interest.

Three, *if your family can be there for you, let them know what you need and exactly how they can help.* Families change over the years. Sadly, many people continue to expect the same reactions from their parents and family that they received twenty years ago. This may not be fair. When was the last time you told your parents exactly what you needed? Have you told them how you would like them to listen to you?

Four, *follow through with creating the most nurturing and satisfying relationship possible.* Be prepared for some setbacks and less than perfect results. But you may be able to create something good and rewarding. Perhaps your family can give you some of the things you ask for, but not all. Keep doing your part.

Finally, *if your family cannot be there for you, create a new family.* Choose a set of friends that can create a multi-legged stool to keep you propped up. Carefully select those people you know will love you through this crisis. Don't rely too much on any one person, but choose a "family" of friends that will be there for you in your times of distress.

## Children Caught in the Middle

While your pain throughout this ordeal is undoubtedly central in your mind, you also realize that you are not the only one affected by the loss of the stability, safety, and constancy of the family. You are keenly aware that your children have been left exposed to the profound shock of lost love and possible separation from one parent. You know that your moods and actions cascade through the family and that your children do not have the resources to protect themselves as you do. Let's consider the world of the child and the impact of marital instability on them.

Children, by virtue of their age and innocence, cannot process what is happening. Their level of distress is magnified by their confusion at being unable to understand what is taking place. While many, especially at early ages, cannot understand what is happening, they can feel it. Let's consider some of the reactions you can expect from your children. First, *children are apt to wonder about things and ask questions.* They wonder about everything that they see. They are naturally curious and want explanations. They wonder, Why is Daddy leaving home? Why is Mommy crying so much? Why can't we keep living together? Their world is collapsing, and they cannot make sense of it. They only see the obvious: One parent is moving out and one parent is staying in the house. This does not make sense to them.

A woman I was working with recently said that her bright young daughter wondered why her dad didn't want to be with her anymore. The mother was at a loss to explain the situation. Of course, her husband did want to see his daughter, but he was caught up in the process of moving to another home and separating from his wife. This, combined with his work, left little extra time for his children.

Second, *children ask questions when you don't have the answers.* One of the primary difficulties is that they will be wondering about these things at the same time you are trying desperately to cope with them yourself. Many times the last thing you want or need is your child asking questions about your marriage and the family. You are feeling vulnerable and do not need additional challenges. Yet your children, of course, are not able to understand your condition any more than they understand what is happening to them.

The mother mentioned previously desperately wanted to answer her daughter's questions, but she had few answers. She did not know if her husband would be coming back

home. She did not know when he would make time to see
their children.

Third, *your children may attempt to protect you.* Children
seem to have radar. While they cannot necessarily process
things intellectually, they can sense tension and uncertainty.
Sensing your vulnerability, children often try to comfort
their hurting parents. It can be a precious thing to see, yet
it is not good for children to feel responsible for the happiness of their parents. The burden is far too large for their
frail shoulders.

Having said that, let's remember that this is not a perfect
world. You cannot expect yourself to be perfectly composed
during this very difficult time. Your life has probably been
turned upside down, and you cannot act as if nothing is
happening. The kids will see you cry, get angry, lose your
car keys, and unravel at times. However, they are not going
to be damaged by simply seeing you being real.

Trisha's two sons saw her crying on a number of occasions and attempted to comfort her. At first she tried to tell
them that nothing was wrong, but that did not feel right to
her. Eventually she told them how sad she was that she and
their father were no longer living together. That felt more
honest and real to her—and to them.

Fourth, *children are easily put into the middle.* Children,
because they desire to understand, may at times ask questions that should not be answered. Full of natural curiosity,
they will ask questions about your situation, your mood,
or what is happening. You should not give them more
information than they need. Children's lives are meant to
be relatively carefree, unencumbered by the problems of

adulthood. Your children are not the mediators between you and your partner.

Children will ask questions that will trigger bad feelings on your part. "Did Daddy really leave for another woman?" "Don't you love Mommy anymore?" "Why can't you just move back with Mommy?" These questions can be answered in a way that will be helpful to your children or in a way that will be damaging. For example, if indeed he has fallen in love with another woman, they can be told that by your husband when he is ready to share that information. Share the truth appropriately with their level of maturity. It will do no good for you to make derogatory comments about this other person. Children should also be told the truth about the possibilities of reconciliation as soon as you know it. If you do not know the outcome of your marriage, you need to say that to them to avoid creating false expectations and hopes.

Fifth, *children should not be told anything derogatory about the other parent.* A general guideline is that saying anything inflammatory about your spouse will not be helpful. This will only serve to alienate the child from that parent and encourage them to take sides. Avoid the temptation. Do everything possible not to succumb to your desire to speak badly about your spouse.

Take caution not to ask them what they know about your spouse's activities. This is information that they will likely be sensitive about sharing. Children are perceptive and easily feel stuck in the middle between their parents.

Sixth, *if there has been a separation, children will have fantasies about reconciliation.* Most children simply cannot fathom the concept of their parents being apart. A family is meant to be together, and that is the hard and fast reality for them.

Ellen Sue Stern, in talking about children's reactions to parents' separations, says, "Most kids have secret fantasies, hopes, and dreams of their parents getting back together. It's hard to believe that they're really going through this—it takes some time for the reality to sink in. Until it does, you [children] may go back and forth between 'getting it' and thinking there's no way this could really be happening."[1]

Given that children are likely to have unrealistic fantasies about the separation, it will be important to *give them accurate information that is appropriate to their age and ability to understand.* Tell them, if you know, how long you might be away from their other parent. Tell them how often they will be able to see their other parent. Let them know what they can expect.

Seventh, *children will struggle with the instability of the situation and need as much constancy as possible, just like you.* Though your life has been turned upside down and you have no idea what to cook for dinner tonight, your kids still need *constancy and predictability.* They need to have routines and structure to guide their lives. They need to be in their own beds each night if possible. If they must be transported between two homes, it is critical that they have some of their favorite things and familiar belongings at both homes. It is no fun for your kids to live out of a suitcase. Ideally, if they are young, they should spend the majority of their time at their primary home.

Finally, *your children need both of you.* Be careful that any hostile feelings you have toward your spouse are not displaced onto your children. Don't use your children as a pawn to punish your spouse. If you do vent your ill feelings toward your spouse, you make that parent partially unavailable to the child. Your children will begin to take on your feelings, and this separates them from the other parent. I don't think you truly want that to happen. That will only add to their hurt and confusion.

## What Kids Want to Say to Their Parents

While children often have trouble saying what they would like to say about what is happening around them, they do have feelings about it. They can sense the changes occurring in the family. Here are a couple of statements from children concerning what they would like to say to their parents on the issue of separation. Perhaps they echo what your children might like to say to you.

You should try to get your kids to understand that it's not their fault. When my family was separated, I felt like half my life was torn away and that I would never be happy again. But my parents say that they will still be friends and that they will both see us equally.[2]

I think kids really want a family with two parents. My mom lives in another town. She goes to school. And sometimes people tease me about that. I'm kind of mad at my mom for not talking to me and my little brother and my big brother. I suggest that moms or dads talk to their kids.[3]

The night my parents actually separated my screams were so loud our neighbors thought there was a robber at our house. When my parents divorced I went to therapy for 3 years. This summer I'm going to visit my dad for a month and 2 weeks.[4]

These excerpts reveal the fragile hearts of children. They show us how much they can be hurt by parents who have a fractured marriage. They should serve to warn us to be careful with our children, giving them special attention and support during these difficult times.

## Summary

Having a partner tell you that they "don't feel the same way" they used to is very painful. It starts a series of reactions, actions, and decisions that will likely change your life forever. You, your spouse, your children, and your extended family will be intimately impacted.

Losing part of your extended family along with your spouse may be something that you had not anticipated. Furthermore, without good boundaries, your family can get sucked into the middle of the emotional drama of your separation. Guard your heart and emotions to save yourself and your family from additional problems. You have enough on your plate without having to expend energy sorting out family feelings.

Consider carefully the role you wish your family to play in your struggles and how to help your children face this crisis. Using wisdom now will save you and your children many problems later, especially if you and your mate are able to resolve your difficulties and reconcile.

# 8

## SEARCHING
## FOR SILVER

*I am not afraid of storms, for I am*
*learning how to sail my ship.*

Louisa May Alcott

I arrive at my office every day prepared to face an array of problems, and I realize we all face suffering of some kind in life. All of us will struggle with grief and loss. That is the nature of our fallen world, and we must first and foremost come to terms with this reality: No one is exempt from the ravages of pain.

*Life is difficult.* These words, made famous by M. Scott Peck in his book *The Road Less Traveled,* are certainly true. Listen to nearly anyone tell the story of their journey, and you will hear words of loss and gain, pain and pleasure. Life is a mosaic of experiences, some good, others bad. We all know this to be true.

In *The Road Less Traveled,* Dr. Peck takes a turn on us. Just when we think he is going to sympathize with our plights, he makes the case that we complain too much, too often. He even says that what we complain about is not the real issue. He asserts that much of our problem lies in the fact that we expect life to be pleasant and then are shocked when troubles come our way. "Most do not fully see this truth that life is difficult," Peck says. "Instead they moan more or less incessantly, noisily or subtly, about the enormity of their problems, their burdens, and their difficulties as if life were generally easy, as if life *should* be easy."[1]

His words feel a bit brutal to me—perhaps because I am very much like the people he describes in the previous paragraph. I don't always want to hear the truth. I want to find a friend who will let me complain and whine a bit. But if Dr. Peck's words lack empathy, they surely do not lack candor.

Dr. Peck's position is not new. In fact, if you listen carefully to his words, you will hear an echo from the apostle James. The book of James is replete with assertions that we must make peace with our struggles, for they will be with us a long while. We are encouraged to lean into troubles and to see them as a source of instruction and growth. "Consider it pure joy, my brothers, whenever you face trials of many kinds, because you know that the testing of your faith develops perseverance. Perseverance must finish its work so that you may be mature and complete, not lacking anything" (James 1:2–4). Again, these are not the words I like to hear. How dare James say that we should feel good, even joyful, about times of trial?

Times of marital adversity certainly constitute times of trials. Even if you saw it coming, even if you have had ample time to adjust to the breakdown in the relationship, something is terribly bewildering about the breakup of a marriage. For some, the emotional impact is tantamount to the death of a loved one. But James was right. In spite of the pain and confusion, this traumatic time has the power to instruct us and make us wiser. Silver can be found in this minefield if we are careful, observant, and open to new possibilities.

## The Search for Silver

Right after James talks about the benefits of trials, he adds these words: "If any of you lacks wisdom, he should ask God, who gives generously to all without finding fault, and it will be given to him" (James 1:5). James seems to be saying that in order to face life's trials effectively, we must add wisdom to our toolbox. We must be careful to avoid a myopic point of view but instead pull out our field glasses and scan the horizon for lessons amid the pain.

This process of searching for valued lessons is most bewildering when you are still flinching from the loss of someone you have loved. Still, the blessings are there. Dr.

John DeMartini says in his book *Count Your Blessings*, "Just because you can't see the blessings of your heartache doesn't mean they're not there. The events and circumstances in our lives that offer the most heartache also offer the greatest opportunities to experience the magnificence of unconditional love and the perfection of the universe. . . . Even the deepest, darkest sorrows have an equal amount of joy—the sooner we find it, the sooner we experience the blessings."[2]

Searching for lessons in adversity can be similar to searching for silver in a pile of sediment. Silver has many wonderful uses and is often classified with gold and platinum as a precious metal. But for our purposes, silver is the deep wisdom and character refinement we seek to guide us on our path.

Silver is rare and difficult to obtain. But Solomon says that it does not have to be that hard. Silver can be found by simply asking the right person for directions. He says, "If you call out [to the Lord] for insight and cry aloud for understanding, and if you look for it as for silver and search for it as for hidden treasure, then you will understand the fear of the LORD" (Prov. 2:3–5).

The search for silver will take you into precarious territory, so you must be careful. Just as the cautious sailor does not venture far into wild winds and waves, so too the seeker of silver does not meander into mines that are on the verge of a cave-in. The search for silver must be done cautiously and with forethought. We must be prepared to dig deep within our circumstances and ourselves if we are to mine the valuable experience for the hidden silver—the lessons learned only through adversity.

## The Silversmith

The silversmith, like the sailor, works with raw elements of nature. Wind and water can chill and kill, but fire can burn. The silversmith knows this and has an incredible respect for the elements. He has patience as he approaches the fiery furnace.

The silversmith works in a delicate balance. Alertness is important, as is attitude. The silversmith knows that the silver must be refined, but this is a tedious and temperamental process. First he must place the silver into a very hot furnace. He cannot take his eye off the molten material. Left in the fire too long, the silver would be destroyed. But it must be left in long enough to burn off the impurities. When does he know it is refined enough? When he can see his reflection in the silver.

The Lord uses all life experiences, even love lost, to refine our lives. He wants to see his reflection in us. Understanding and accepting this refining process can transform utter agony into a purposeful and rewarding struggle. Listen to the prophet Malachi talk about the Lord's refining fire:

> For he will be like a refiner's fire or a launderer's soap. He will sit as a refiner and purifier of silver; he will purify the Levites and refine them like gold and silver. Then the LORD will have men who will bring offerings in righteousness, and the offerings of Judah and Jerusalem will be acceptable to the LORD, as in days gone by, as in former years.
>
> Malachi 3:2–4

Surely the Levites did not welcome these words. Surely they, like us, asked if there could be another way. Perhaps they said, "Please, Lord, turn the heat down. We promise we'll pay attention this time." But the Lord knew then, as he knows now, what he was doing. He knew that to be refined into purity required a fiery experience.

Do you feel like you are going through such an experience? Perhaps it is for the purpose of your refining.

## Cathy's Depression

Cathy was a forty-year-old homemaker who had been given the news that her husband, Jerry, wanted out of their twenty-year marriage. Her life had been a tapestry of soccer practice and piano lessons for the kids, choir practice for herself, and cooking and household chores. She relished her life and saw no appeal in the hectic lives of friends who worked outside the home.

She loved the children but was looking forward to the years when she and Jerry, a successful building contractor, would use the money they had been saving to travel. She had also begun to think about taking an evening class to learn more about oil painting, a passion she had never had much time to pursue. She could see the day when she would have a bit more money and much more time. She had hoped that the added time would also give her a chance to become closer to Jerry.

Everything changed with five horrible words: "I don't love you anymore." With those words Jerry radically altered the road map of their lives. He had apparently quit thinking about how they might renew their relationship after the children were out of the home. His hopes and dreams no longer included her.

Jerry could not, or would not, explain his feelings to her. He simply kept repeating, "This is not what I want anymore." The relationship lacked the zest he was searching for, and he was not inclined to rebuild it. He too was in turmoil, he reassured her, and this decision was not an easy one for him. His road map for the future was as fuzzy as hers. But he had made up his mind.

With three adolescents in the home and no marketable skills, Cathy panicked. In fact, when her husband delivered the announcement, she felt as if her world was collapsing around her. "What do you mean?" she kept asking him, as if he what he was saying might not be real. His words seemed impossible to comprehend.

Cathy did not call for an appointment with me right away. Stunned and confused, she later told me that she had wandered around the house for weeks trying to make sense out of the situation. Jerry's decision to end their marriage was the last thing she had expected. She could not think straight or make any meaningful decision, let alone call for help. By the time I saw her, she had lost ten pounds and hadn't had a good night's sleep in a month.

I sat quietly with Cathy and let her talk about their marriage and what this loss meant for her. Her husband was resolute about ending the marriage. He refused to attend marriage counseling and did not want to talk to their pastor. In fact, after he told her of his decision, he had quickly moved out. She had little time to prepare or even talk to him about his seemingly rash move. She was left empty and confused.

At first Cathy seemed to slip into a depression. Feeling despondent was certainly an honest response to such an enormous loss. Grief compounded can take on qualities usually seen in the diagnosis of depression. For weeks she had no appetite, her sleep was fitful at best, and her energy had vanished. She lacked hope and feared her future. She admitted that for a few moments she had felt suicidal, though she no longer felt that way. Yet her life had been completely wrapped up in being a mother and wife, and she could see no way to rebuild it.

"There will be time to rebuild your life," I said. "For now, your task is to grieve. It is to simply reflect and to start sleeping and eating again. Later will be time to begin the process of rebuilding."

As the weeks went by, Cathy did regain her strength. She dug deeply to find the resolve to go on, though not without moments of wanting to end everything. Slowly she began to face the immediate tasks of creating a new life.

"You have a huge task ahead of you," I said. "You do not need to do everything at once, but gradually you will need to find some meaning in what has happened to you. You will need to find the lessons that are hidden in this tragedy. This is a time to grab hold of your faith and see what God has in store for you."

For the moment, Cathy was frozen. Stepping back and seeing things from a larger perspective takes time. She needed more time to be able to begin to decide how to move forward with her life.

As time slowly offered Cathy perspective and healing, she gradually began to see that she could move through this massive grief. She was able to see that she still had a lot to live for and many goals she still wanted to pursue in her life. With counseling and some medications to help her get the rest she desperately needed, she began the arduous task of putting a new life back together.

## Jerry's Life

When we hear Cathy's story and consider the many other women and men who have been abandoned, we are tempted to empathize only with her. We want to yell at Jerry to go back home and work things out with Cathy. His children still need him, and his wife is ill-equipped to face the world alone. He should be there to support and love them. But, as always, the story has another side. Things are rarely as simple as they seem.

As we peek into Jerry's life, we find him living in a one-bedroom apartment. This is hardly the life he imagined for himself at this stage of his career. He had spent years building a wonderful home for his family, and he felt intense pangs of guilt and sadness when he watched it disappear from his rearview mirror. He left a beautiful home in the country for an apartment in the city. Why? Many people seem to attribute his decision to mid-life crisis and say he will "come to his senses" before long. He resents their quick, uninformed opinions about him as well as the embellished rumors that seem rampant.

Jerry has been unhappy for years. As is typical for many men, he hid his depression. He worked long hours to bring home a paycheck that never seemed to stretch as long as the month. He felt unappreciated. He thought that he and Cathy had far less intimacy in their relationship than he desired, but he did not know how to share his feelings.

As the years went by, the distance grew between Cathy and him. She was unaware that he had begun harboring resentment and was planning a better life without her. He had little idea what that life might look like, but he was determined now to find it. His sparsely decorated apartment seemed like a terrible way to start again, but he felt guilty for his decision to leave and wanted his wife to have enough money and the stability of their home. However meager his life, he reasoned that it was better than what he had left behind.

Jerry finds it hard to articulate what was so bad about the life he left. He only knows that he has been unhappy for a long time, though has rarely verbalized it. He put most of his energies into his job, and lately even that has been less than satisfying. Perhaps he is experiencing the mid-life crisis that his friends and co-workers have pointed to as the reason behind his action. Perhaps he will "come to his senses" and go back home. For now, however, he wants to stay in this newly created world apart from his wife. He sees his children regularly and is not considering a new relationship. He wants time to reflect and is giving Cathy little hope for the future. This will be a painful time of waiting for both.

## A Matter of Perspective

Only those who have experienced lost love and possible marital separation coupled with the threat of impending divorce can know the depths of pain associated with the struggle. Those who have been in that place know the sheer agony of watching a spouse walk out the door into the arms of another lover or the dread of knowing that you will soon be facing a life of uncertainty and darkness. Perhaps you have walked out of a familiar home, left a familiar life with known expectations, and entered a world filled with doubt and confusion. In either case, the attitude you carry with you will make all the difference.

People commonly leave a marriage feeling as though they have been ripped off and are the complete victim of the situation. While this is sometimes true, rarely are things so cut-and-dried. Gaining a new perspective will mean letting go of the indulgence of feeling like the victim. Yes, you are entitled to your season of pain and grief, and you need to lean into that as well. But soon you will need to shift positions and begin to examine your part in this situation. Only when you do that will you be able to learn from it.

Ever since the days of Adam and Eve, we have been hurling insults and hiding from responsibility. We have projected blame onto others and found temporary comfort in seeing ourselves as innocent bystanders. Rarely is a marital breakup a one-sided situation.

Take a moment to do some soul-searching. Ask yourself the following questions:

- What was my part in this breakup?
- What do I need to take responsibility for, and what does my mate need to own?
- How could I have done things differently?
- What would I like to learn from this situation?

If you answer those questions honestly, you will be well on your way toward gaining a new and beneficial perspective. Being the victim keeps us trapped and feeling powerless. Sure, we will get some strokes from our friends, but we will also be left feeling empty and stuck. Rehearsing our victimization again and again is resentment, which has little value. We need to move forward, and taking responsibility is the first, most powerful step.

Are you ready to take hold of your life and look for the silver lining on this dark cloud? Perspective is everything. The proper attitude will be the difference between purposeless agony and the gritty endurance needed to finish the race and accept your prize. You are running a marathon, and there *will* be a prize at the finish, I assure you.

Joseph Stowell, in his helpful book *Through the Fire,* assists us with the needed attitude change. He asserts that pain will either make us or break us, and he insists that the choice is ours. None of us wants to be broken by our circumstances. We want to have the courage to lean into our painful situation and mine all the silver we can from it. What attitude shift is necessary, according to Stowell?

First, he says, we need to understand the certainty that "*everything that comes into our lives comes through the sovereign permission of God.* . . . Nothing—absolutely nothing—passes into our lives that has not passed by the sovereign authority of God. He is the divine sentinel."[3]

Stowell goes on to illustrate this truth by detailing the story of Job. Job had been creating a very prosperous life for himself until Satan came to God and claimed that Job's allegiance to God was only the result of being protected and blessed. God decided to allow incredible adversity into Job's life to show Satan that Job would still give glory to God. Though his wife encouraged him to curse God and die, Job was dedicated to God. While he lost his family and bountiful life and suffered horrifically, he still vowed allegiance to the Lord. Ultimately his life became prosperous again, but through the entire ordeal God was the divine sentinel in Job's life, just as he is in ours.

Second, Stowell notes that *we must cling to God's promises if we are to make it through the process intact.* What are some promises that can help you deal with your suffering? Perhaps the most powerful truth that you can grab hold of at this time is that your pain has a purpose. Reflect on this passage from the apostle Paul:

> And we know that in all things God works for the good of those who love him, who have been called according to his purpose.
>
> Romans 8:28

We can find such comfort in these words if we will believe them and let them transform our lives. Let's pull this verse apart for a few moments.

*For we know.* Wow! At a time when your emotions are swirling around you like a whirlpool, when one moment you can be laughing and the next crying, it is good to *know* something.

Some of you are hard-wired to be very emotional—like me. I feel things deeply. I care for people deeply and am hurt deeply when relationships are damaged. I have to stretch to remind myself that some truths stand regardless of how

I am feeling. *For we know* is a good place to start the healing process.

Now, what can you know? The next line adds *that all things*. Not just some of the more obvious lessons in life are meant for our good. All things, including this marital pain, have the potential for positive results.

If you are like me, you may be asking God, "Do you really mean *all things*? Are you sure, God, that you don't mean *most things*? How can something as rotten as a separation be helpful to my character?" Well, he said *all* things, and that means all things.

The next line is interesting too. All things *work together*. Could this possibly mean that all of my history and all of my future is knitted together in one carefully crafted tapestry? I believe that is the case.

*For good!* Yes, all things are working together for good. You will look back on this painful process and, if you allow the Potter to do his masterful work, see a fine image emerge.

I am reminded of the words of the prophet Jeremiah, which have often encouraged me in times of struggle. I know they were penned by the Holy Spirit to encourage all of us today.

> "For I know the plans I have for you," declares the LORD,
> "plans to prosper you and not to harm you, plans to give
> you hope and a future. Then you will call upon me and
> come and pray to me, and I will listen to you. You will
> seek me and find me when you seek me with all your
> heart."
>
> Jeremiah 29:11–13

Can you believe that the pain-wracked life you are living now has a purpose? Can you believe that good will flow from it? Will you search diligently for the silver in the process? Have faith in a positive outcome, and your life will be transformed.

Certainly Cathy and Jerry must apply these truths to their lives. They will need to take hold of the basic principles of their faith to lead them through this incredible time of uncertainty. They will need to believe that whatever happens in their marriage, God is not finished with them. They will face lessons learned and opportunities for greater intimacy with God.

## Pain Is a Process

People experiencing marital rejection feel a profound sense of injustice. One man I worked with recently talked about feeling his pain palpably, as if he were moving on a conveyor belt through something he could not define. He was uncertain about what had been real and true in his life, was unable to articulate what he was experiencing, and was very confused as to what might be coming next. He also went through what is often called the "dark night of the soul" where God too seems to be absent.

Where are the guides for this process? At times you will undoubtedly feel very alone in your search for silver. You will feel like you are not doing enough. You will tell yourself that there must be something more proactive that you can do to bring about a satisfactory outcome.

During a particularly stressful time in my life I went away to a retreat center to be alone and pray and to meet with a spiritual director. As I poured out my tale of woe, I pressed her for answers. I wanted to *do something* to get rid of my pain. And I wanted to do it immediately. I wanted clear assignments that would help me alleviate my problems. Her advice was simple and disquieting. She suggested that I *not work on the problem, but let the problem work on me.*

Most of us would rather just face the demons and get on with life. We are uncomfortable in the process and would gladly bypass the refining fire. But it is as we go *through* the pain that we grow. We all have a variety of ways to avoid the grief associated with separation, but if we will lean into the struggle and endure the sadness, loneliness, injustice, and fear, we will come out on the other side feeling renewed and energized.

Alexandra Stoddard, in her book *The Art of the Possible,* discusses this issue of accepting change and in fact leaning into it. She says that it is here, in the acceptance of our changing lives, that we are able to discover joy. "We must balance our attachment to the things we love with the ability to let go. We know that many essential things will change: we will grow old, we will lose friends and family, and we may face opposition. But, regardless of whether the change is, on the surface, good or bad, accepting it will surely help us grow spiritually—and that is always a plus."[4]

Though it may seem at times like God is painfully quiet, if you listen carefully you will hear his voice. He has not abandoned you. Crises are spiritually rich times in our lives. When we can no longer rely on our own resources to pull

us through, we are more apt to trust that God is in control
and has our best in mind.

## Expecting Growth

As you move through your current difficulties you can,
as we have discussed, lean into the struggle and expect
growth to happen. In fact, if you expect growth and look
for the silver, you are far more likely to find it. But you must
be open to finding it, sometimes in unexpected places.

In an entertaining book titled *When God Winks,* Squire
Rushnell challenges us to look for the little gifts from God
in unusual places. Although I was initially skeptical of this
suggestion, I have been delighted with the results. When I
am open to seeing little gifts from God every day, in whatever form or fashion he chooses, I am not disappointed.
But I must be receptive.

Just the other day it "just so happened" that on a deserted
country road I hit a huge pothole which flattened my two
right tires. It "just so happened" that I had a speaking en-
gagement thirty minutes later in a town twenty miles away.
As I got out of my car to inspect the damage and moan about
my plight, it "just so happened" that the next car was driven
by an elderly woman who never stops to pick up strangers.
It "just so happened" that she was going to the same town
to have lunch with a friend and would take me there. It
"just so happened" that I arrived to give my talk with five
minutes to spare.

Do you remember the story, told in John 5, of the lame
man who spent thirty-eight years lying beside the pool of
healing waters? This weary, woeful individual cannot seem

to get his life together. His life is defined by his problems. He *is* a lame man!

But the story takes an interesting turn. Jesus asks the man, "Do you want to be healed?" The man had to wonder if Jesus was being sarcastic or just didn't understand his plight. Of course he wanted to be healed! At least that was what he believed and wanted others to believe. He had spent the most productive years of his life lying beside that pool, a helpless invalid.

Author Terry Hershey, considering Jesus' seemingly ridiculous question, suggests the following: "Perhaps Jesus asks the question because He knew a fundamental truth about human nature: the presence of sickness does not automatically bring a desire for healing. The presence of a problem such as divorce (or separation) does not automatically bring a desire for growth and change."[5]

The man offered a raft of excuses for why he could not get healed. Do we approach some of our problems the same way? Do we cling to our problems rather than look for the solutions? Do we expect to grow through our problems? Do we look for the hidden gifts that God offers as part of our growth process?

Those who expect good things to happen in their lives are far happier than those who expect only calamity. Those who see challenges as opportunities for growth are often pleasantly correct. The difference is whether you approach life's trials as a victim or as a victor. I often challenge my clients not to limit themselves, or God, by viewing their struggle from a victim's perspective. We are far more empowered by looking for the "God winks" in even our most troubling situation.

## Enjoying the Silver

It seems to me that if we are going to go through the pain and process of mining the silver, we might as well enjoy the final product. And why not? Searching for silver is tough work, not for the faint-hearted. When we find the silver we should enjoy it, embrace it, wear it like a skillfully carved bracelet. Silver is one of the many gifts our Creator has given generously to us. The discoveries you are making on this perilous trip through lost love are also to be enjoyed, if you will take the time to do so.

Alexandra Stoddard illustrates this with another story of transition, the story of how she reluctantly gave up an interior design job she had enjoyed for years. After much deliberation she gave up her plush office and many other benefits in exchange for a chance to venture out on her own. This was a difficult decision for her. She had many positive relationships at her workplace. But it was time for a change. She gave up many things to start her own firm, but the result was much better than she could have anticipated. Having gone through "the fire," she now enjoys running her own firm. What assisted her through the process? Listen to her philosophy on change and enjoying the resulting silver:

> My experience encourages me to believe that if we accept change, we can continue to deepen ourselves, to unfold, to discover fresh curiosities, to appreciate all the opportunities, and to accept our limitations, our necessary compromises, and even accept our mortality. Think about a river. See how it flows with tributaries running off. Water must have this

freedom to go its course. When it doesn't, it overflows and
erodes the land. Water is always moving, or it stagnates.
We need the same freedom to flow, to let go, to move and
refresh ourselves.[6]

Now you may be thinking that Alexandra Stoddard wasn't
dumped; she chose her fate. This may pale in comparison
to being rejected or having left a long-term relationship.
But the principles are much the same. Though you may not
have chosen your situation, you now decide how you will
face the trials that come your way. You can choose how fluid
you want to be. The choice of how to respond is a powerful
antidote to discouragement.

## Summary

Fresh, flowing, restorative water—consider the image, for
it is one that can offer us encouragement. Your task today
is to let the changes taking place in your life flow through
you. Develop an attitude of openness to change. Always
remain aware of the new opportunities and gifts that can
rise from that change.

Pain is never enjoyable. No one likes to lean into the
struggles of their lives. Relationship loss is a grueling process
for most, an endurable problem for some. Viktor Frankl, the
famous Swiss analyst, is reported to have said that suffering
ceases to be suffering if there is meaning to it. That surely
seems to be true. But remember that finding the meaning in
your particular difficulty is a challenge that belongs solely
to you. Reframing the agony into a learning experience is
your test.

The Scriptures are clear, and time certainly reveals, that we will have hardship in this life. But we can also find deeper meaning if we are willing to search for it. We can find the silver in the mud and debris. But we must have open eyes and a receptive heart. Blessings to you as you courageously search for your own silver.

# 9

CRUCIBLE
FOR CHANGE

*All rising to a great place is by a*
*winding stair.*

Francis Bacon

Jack sat across from me, looking perturbed. He had been
separated from Barbara, his wife of seven years, for over
nine months now and still knew very little about where he
was going with his life. He was a successful businessman,
a decisive, no-nonsense type of guy. He was accustomed
to being in control. The uncertainty about his future with
Barbara was a source of consternation for him. He wanted
his life to be wrapped up in a neat package, but he was

discovering that what he wanted was not necessarily what he got.

He had not wanted the separation. He had not wanted his wife to busy herself with her career to the point where he felt he had no marriage left. He had asked her repeatedly to slow down, to spend more time at home with him and their three wonderful children. His words seemed to fall on deaf ears. "I went to school to be a professional accountant, and we both knew that it would require an investment of our lives," Barbara had told him. "You knew this when you married me. It's not like you can't understand, since you enjoy your work too."

Still, Jack had believed that after college and giving birth to their children, Barbara would cut back on her hours at the office. He had been willing to slow his life down for the family and expected her to do the same. Surely the demands of the kids' schedules and activities, along with running the home, would have tired her out, he reasoned. But she insisted on more than fifty-hour workweeks, leaving little time for their marriage. He watched helplessly as their relationship withered. Between outbursts he sat quietly, feeling rejected, and began to entertain the unthinkable: an end to their love relationship.

One day Jack finally realized that life was not likely to change without radical intervention. However, he was not prepared for the emotional impact separation would have on his life. When the end came, Jack wanted his life to move forward, like his own professional life. He thought that he had lost his love for his wife but found that he could not quickly scurry past the many memories. These barriers to "progress" were a frustration to him.

Even after many counseling sessions, I couldn't say that Jack had made a lot of progress. He could smile when he talked about his impatience, but then he would launch into a list of reasons why he should be farther along the path of his life. He had little tolerance for being "in between." He just couldn't abide the uncertainty of his life.

Jack really is no different from many others in this situation. Most of us want to keep a road map handy so that we can see where we have been and where we are going, making little notations to ensure that we are making progress. Unfortunately, our lives do not always cooperate with our attempts to map them, and few measurements tell us whether we are ahead of where we were at the same time last month.

## Transitions

Lost love and broken relationships rarely are neat and tidy situations. Rarely does one partner wake up and boldly announce that they have lost all feelings for the other, although certainly this happens. More commonly couples face a period of uncertainty, time spent in the heated crucible where refining takes place. It is awkward and uncomfortable for both parties.

Life offers us transitions, and certainly lost love and possible marital separation constitutes a major life transition. Transitions are no fun. Most of us want to avoid them at any cost. But this isn't possible. Periods of transition have the potential to be some of the most fruitful times of our lives. However, they are also some of the most tormenting times for our souls.

Why are these times of being "in between"—not where we have been or directly heading where we would like to go—so painful? It is because when we are in transition, we are giving up the old life that was so comfortable and predictable. Notice that I did not say it was a happy life or a healthy life. But it was probably predictable. You knew what to expect and how to behave. You were cushioned by comfortable family rituals and routines.

Transitions are a time between one place and another. If you are like me, you are tempted to go back to where you were. You do not want to cross over the bridge of uncertainty into the unknown. Even if the place where I have been is painful, I am reluctant to move forward if I cannot clearly see what lies ahead.

> There is no sin punished more implacably by nature than the sin of resistance to change.
>
> Anne Morrow Lindbergh

Remember the Israelites who were being led out of a land of captivity (see the book of Exodus, especially starting in chapter 12)? They were prisoners—overworked, abused, and mistreated. You would expect them to be horrified at their condition and ready for any form of rescue.

When they finally were allowed to leave Egypt, the land of bondage, they were not taken straight to the Promised Land. They needed to learn some lessons, so God set up a school for them. He did so by arranging a detour, a longer route *through the desert.*

Were the Israelites content to be out of slavery? Hardly. "If only we had died by the LORD's hand in Egypt," they murmured. "There we sat around pots of meat and ate all the food we wanted, but you have brought us out into this desert to starve this entire assembly to death" (Exod. 16:3). So much for gratitude to God for saving their skins! The grumbling and quarreling did not stop there. They spent quite some time in the Mount Sinai School of Hard Knocks, learning their lessons. They did not easily accept that God would provide for their every need on a daily basis.

But lest we quickly judge the Israelites and assume that we would act differently, let me remind you of our own tendency to go back. Back to where things were predictable. Back to where we knew exactly how to behave. Back to where we could feel good about feeling bad. How many of us feel as though we are being taken through the desert on the way to a promised land? *Letting go is hard, hard business.*

## Stages of Transition

When told that we are no longer loved, or when telling a mate that we no longer love them, we set in motion a cascading series of changes. Suddenly we enter a place of transition, a place where we are forced to let go of the familiar and embrace the frightening prospect of the unknown.

Transition is time in the crucible, that place of refining fire where real change occurs. Have you noticed that change generally does not occur when things are bright and rosy in our lives? The good times are wonderful, but they are generally not when we wrestle with the deep, thorny issues of our lives. Why should we? We are relatively content with our circumstances; thus we feel no fire beneath us forcing us to examine our personality conflicts and relationship problems.

You are probably reading this book because your marriage is in a time of transition. Whether you have chosen your course or had it thrust upon you and whether or not you and your partner reconcile, *you will not be the same again.* Transition changes us forever. Like it or not, we cannot return to Egypt. We can travel to a new place that is brighter and better, flowing with milk and honey. But to get to that glorious land, we must pass through the desert of transition.

What does transition look like in our lives? What is the nature of this gritty time when the soul cries out for surrender? William Bridges, author of the wonderful book *The Way of Transition,* outlines several salient traits of change. Consider how you may be experiencing some of these.

*Disengagement:* separation from whatever it is that you have lost

*Disidentification:* the way the loss destroys the old identity you had

*Disenchantment:* the way the loss tears you out of the old reality you accepted unthinkingly

*Disorientation:* feeling bewildered and lost as a result of losing a relationship as well as the identity you had together and the reality you shared

*Discovery:* finding a new life, a new identity, and a new outlook[1]

Let's ponder each of these traits and see how they apply to time in the crucible.

*Disengagement.* Certainly all who have been separated from spouse and family feel the pain of disengagement. Disengagement involves a tearing apart of something, much like a fabric being torn. You remember the feeling and perhaps still have it: the lump in the stomach; tears; anger; wishing to be reunited with the lost one; obsessing about the family being together; feeling guilt over what you may have done to contribute to the problems; and so on.

Disengagement does not happen in a single moment. It is a series of decisions, actions, and events. You may go to certain family affairs now without your spouse. You may choose to celebrate holidays with others. You may or may not be socializing with your spouse. Disengagement is happening, perhaps quite painfully, in a series of steps, large or small. Can you acknowledge the magnitude of the effect of this process on you? This powerful loss is part of the refining fire of the crucible.

This stage of disengagement also could be likened to the desert experience. The Scriptures use the image of the desert as a place where powerful things happen. As you may recall, Jesus' ministry began in the wilderness. There Jesus was tempted by Satan and showed that he was able to overcome evil and temptation. In this desolate place he illustrated that the spiritual life was more important than the desires of the flesh.

M. Robert Muholland speaks eloquently about the desert experience as a powerful place of inner change. "The desert experience begins when something moves us away from the habitual structures of our being and doing and takes us into an alien and hostile environment," he writes. "Perhaps the transition is engendered by a loss, a reversal, a death of someone or something that has been an essential part of our lives."[2]

In this dry and desolate place, among companions of fear and trepidation, you are forced to see the world in new ways. Much of the familiar has been stripped from you, leaving you raw and adrift in the unknown. Muholland states that this arid land is the perfect place for the false self to die. Dramatic personal and spiritual change is possible here as you let go of old notions, habits, and ways of living. But change is never easy.

One woman told me recently that she had an extremely difficult time this past Christmas. Old rituals and habits no longer served her well. She had to decide if she would be with her husband and children. Since she was separated from her husband and things were not going particularly well for them, she chose not to spend the holiday with him. That meant that she had to make extra arrangements for being with their children, ensuring the children had time with their father, and trying to make it the least traumatic possible for everyone involved. In spite of her valiant efforts, it was still a very painful time. She could not make all the pieces of the puzzle come together seamlessly. Why? Because no matter how much we attempt to control the circumstances, disengagement is always painful.

*Disidentification.* Love lost changes many things, including how you see yourself and how you are seen by others. Are you still married? Yes, but you feel differently about the marriage. You have chosen to do something that you may previously have said you would never do—"Till death do us part" was something you believed in, but what do you think now? How has this experience changed your beliefs?

As a separation continues it may alter, on a deeper level, how you view your marriage. Some who have been separated for lengthy periods of time no longer "feel married." They may still honor the vows of marriage, but if they are not in direct contact with their spouse, they may begin to feel quite single. Your identity is being challenged in new ways.

Muholland also talks about the desert being a place where our identity is challenged. Here, he says, the false self will cling tenaciously to old ways of doing and seeing things. He encourages us to stay in the desert and learn necessary lessons. This can be a time when we are able to see ourselves more clearly for who we are. The false self gradually disappears and true motives and values rise to the surface. This can be a time when you let go of shallow, egotistic ideals in favor of deeper spiritual convictions. Jesus said, "If anyone would come after me, he must deny himself and take up his cross and follow me" (Matt. 16:24). This desert can be a place where we lose our identity for the sake of Christ.

In spite of the loss, the challenge to your identity can actually be a good thing. While understandably disquieting and perhaps downright frightening, it provides an opportunity to reflect upon who you really are.

*Disenchantment.* Oh, how it hurts to let go of illusions that we have held onto dearly for many years. Deep within our souls stir notions of romance and dreams come true. But interruptions in our fantasy life bring the rationalism of adulthood crashing in like a flood. A major crisis like a marital separation will give you a potent dose of reality, sullying the beautiful images of innocent, romantic enchantment. These are still dreams that die hard. And they should die hard. Enchantment is a wonderful thing and, in my opinion, should never totally go away. The problem is that enchantment does not easily abide reality. In one form or another, we are disappointed. Lost love and possible marital separation leave us with an empty feeling in the pit of the stomach. Let's listen to Sherrie talk about her disenchantment.

"I guess I was raised the old-fashioned way: stay married to one person for life, with never a thought of leaving him. I watched my parents stay married for over fifty years, and I told myself that I would do the same thing. Then the unthinkable happened. My husband told me that he was no longer in love with me. He told me that he had been staying with me for the sake of the kids, but since they were nearly grown he wanted a separation. He told me that he had always felt like I was inferior to him and that he wasn't doing me any favors by staying with me. He reminded me that he lived and worked in a professional world that I couldn't relate to because I was a homemaker. He told me that his friends came from a different world than mine. His words crushed me. I was ready to die, and if it hadn't been for the children I might have done something stupid. I suspected that he was having an affair, but I'll never know the truth about that. He wants time to think it over, but I am not hopeful that he will return to the marriage.

"When I think about what I lost, it is overwhelming to me. Whether we get back together or not, something has been ripped away. I don't know that I could ever trust him again. He has hurt me deeply. I always looked upon marriage as a safe sanctuary where I could relax and be myself. Tough times would come and go, but my marriage would be something that was always stable. I think about the hopes and dreams I had for us as a couple and family. Now those are all in question. I am fearful, and I have never been fearful like this before. What can you trust? Who can you trust? Those are things I wonder about now."

Disenchantment is a thief of sorts. It steals our innocence. It steals the sense of safety that we need to feel free and protected in this world. Disenchantment is the cold, harsh reality of events that awaken us to the darker things that can and do happen in this world. These things wake us up and make us look closer and deeper for other sources of enchantment.

Have you felt disenchanted? What hopes and dreams have been dashed in your marriage? How has this caused you to reorient your life?

*Disorientation.* Suddenly, perhaps in one fell swoop, your world comes crashing down around you. Oh, you may have heard a few distant sirens, a warning here or there, but you were likely not prepared for the full-fledged cataclysm of being alone. So much of your world, your daily life, has been wrapped up in being married. *What is to become of me?* you wonder.

For many, the disorientation comes most swiftly and surely in the form of loneliness. While you may not be truly alone, as you may still have children in the home, a deafening silence remains amidst the clamoring voices. Something is wrong. You are not at peace in your own company, let alone with others.

This may be the first time you have been alone as an adult. You may have had brief periods of solitude in college or after high school, but not like this. Now you are truly alone. You cannot, or perhaps choose not to, go home to your parents. Friends are available, but they have their own lives and you refuse to impose on them. Now you must dig deep within your own reserve to see if you have the tenacity to make it. All of this creates a climate for grief, volatile emotions, and confusion. Such is the nature of disorientation. After all, a broken marriage shatters the lens we use to view the world. Suddenly nothing is in perspective. You have so many questions, so few answers. And meanwhile you are alone with all your pain and ponderings.

*Discovery.* Thankfully, our story does not end on that sour note. Most assuredly, if you do your grief work, you will move through the challenging phases into the light of discovery and new life. Just as surely as spring follows winter, discovery follows the darkest hours of disorientation. In due time the fog will clear and you will see a new vision. But it must come in its own time. It cannot be hurried, prescribed, or dictated, as much as you might wish that weren't so. If you let yourself sit with the struggle, new insights will come to you. And that is what this chapter, and perhaps book, is all about: *discovery.*

*Discovery.* The word has a ring of hope to it. What if you could make it beyond the unsettling phases of disorientation and disenchantment and reach a place of exciting discovery? Can you begin the process of reframing what is happening to you and decide that you will take an active role in your future? Part of that future can be discovery, where you face the uncertainties of life with an attitude of adventure; you are ready to face each new day because you expect good things to happen.

I am reminded of the adventures of Huck in Mark Twain's classic *The Adventures of Huckleberry Finn*. Mischievous and a bit naïve, Huck is not about to let life become too predictable. No way. He left the security of home because it was a painful place for him. He was ready to face the dangers of the river and the unknown world to let go of a life that was not hospitable to him.

Could an adventurous child emerge from your struggle, ready to search for a new world? Imagine that your world is the great Mississippi, and you have never traveled down this river before. Everything is new, but instead of being afraid, you turn your fear into excitement. What have you seen so far that is interesting to you? What feelings have you had that have surprised you?

I know a woman who is in the midst of a painful separation. I am impressed with her resilience in the face of suffering. One of her tools for coping is to use what she calls "surprising curiosity." Each day, she is open to new things and people that will come into her life. Life is one big adventure, and she is excited to see what each new day will bring. She is ready to see what God will do and how he will do it. This is the wildness and the unpredictable beauty of discovery.

## The Crucible

Having considered the various aspects of transition, let's now turn our focus to the place in which the transition occurs: *the crucible*. A crucible is a ceramic container where chemicals and heat can be combined to form new creations. It is a place of incredible creativity and transformation.

Picture with me the setting of the crucible: the laboratory. It appears to be a rather dry and sterile environment. It is anything but that, for in the crucible things change and are developed. For things to change, however, there must be an alchemical process, where the nature of something is transformed so dramatically that it no longer resembles its previous form and in fact is not structurally the same as before. It has undergone a basic and dramatic change.

*He that lacks time to mourn, lacks time to mend.*

William Shakespeare

That is the promise of the Lord for us if we will submit to the transformational process. Christ himself had many times in the crucible. His most dramatic time in the fire, of course, was on the cross. Here we see the Son of God in a desert experience like no other. Abandoned, alone, and in agony, he could do little but wait and pray. He prayed for himself and others, waiting for the "fire" to do its final work—atonement for the sins of the world and the reconciliation of a lost world to God. From his personal fire Christ would emerge glorified, with a new body, and be reunified with his heavenly Father. The crucible had done its work.

The varied stages of love lost mimic being in a heated crucible. In this place of disengagement and disorientation, you have an opportunity to take a critical look at your life. It is a time rich with possibilities. Left without your comfortable underpinnings for support, you are forced to look heavenward. Under the heat of the "refining fire," the impurities can be burned off. Something new and exciting has the opportunity to emerge. This is the perfect environment for God, the great chemist, to do his great work. Will you let him?

You may be saying, "Hold on. I'm not up for changing completely. I rather liked many parts of my old life. I just want to get rid of the pain, not my identity." That's okay. In this time of alchemical transformation you will not give up the essential qualities that make you unique. Those enduring and delightful qualities will remain. But in the transformational process, you can rid yourself of many insecurities and troubling personality traits, if you will allow it. You will mature like no other time in your life and, in the process, take on the likeness of Christ. Could you get excited about that?

> *The shell must be cracked apart if what is in it is to come out, for if you want the kernel, you must break the shell.*
>
> Meister Eckhart

I am reminded of a middle-aged woman named Delores who had spent several years in the crucible. She had endured a difficult marriage to her husband, Dean, where she suffered rampant emotional abuse. Dean was controlling and demanding and put her down consistently. When she asserted herself he would become threatened and find some way to attack her flagging confidence. He would apologize after repeated bouts of anger but showed little willingness to truly change.

Sadly, Delores's husband was not interested in doing the rigorous work required for personal change. While he was willing to come to counseling for a short time, when the time came for making changes, he dropped out. Delores persisted in doing her work. She refused to let his insecurities pull her down any longer. She worked very hard to develop her character, which gave her tremendous confidence. In a few short years, she completed her bachelor's degree, found a wonderful job, and prepared to leave her marriage.

*I tell you the truth, unless a kernel of wheat falls to the ground and dies, it remains only a single seed. But if it dies, it produces many seeds.*

John 12:24

At this time Delores is not sure what she will do in her marriage. But she is sure that she no longer will tolerate emotional abuse. She is living alone while Dean considers his motivation for real change. She, in turn, is still working on setting healthy boundaries, learning assertiveness skills, and grieving the years of pain associated with her marriage. She wanted to leap out of the crucible many times and go back to the old ways of relating to her husband. But she resisted those temptations. She remained in the crucible and has emerged from the crucible fire a happier person.

### Avoidance of the Crucible

Most of us resist change. We avoid the crucible. It is pretty hot in there, and we are not in control. We would rather dwell in the muddle we know than go to a better place filled with uncertainty. Let's consider some of the quick fix remedies we use to avoid the refining fire of the crucible.

*Busyness.* How many of us are guilty of keeping our calendars overflowing so that we do not have to deal with our pain? You may find it easy, during this challenging time, to spend more time at the office, run more errands, stay more busy than usual. Although darting through life is a sure way to avoid the deeper realities, try to leave space in your day to *just be*. As the saying goes, instead of human *doing*, try human *being*.

*Excessive thinking*. While thinking is usually good, we can spend so much time trying to figure things out that we don't allow ourselves to simply feel our pain. Spend time listening to your body and your heart. Pay attention to what they may be saying to you.

*Eating*. Many people try to anesthetize their pain by filling their painful places with food. Food has long been known to be a soothing comfort to our aching hearts. But, sadly, all it does is take away the pain momentarily, in addition to saddling us with unhealthy pounds and a hefty dose of guilt.

*Drugs*. Some have used a variety of prescribed and non-prescribed drugs to mitigate their pain. I am not opposed to using drugs that have been prescribed as necessary for a particular difficulty. But we must not use such drugs in a manner that is not recommended or take something that has not been prescribed for us. Consider living a little closer to your pain—not running when your grief resurfaces. Let your grief be "the healing feeling."

*Romance and sex*. Remember the dangers of romance that comes too soon after a separation. Romance is a powerful narcotic for pain. Nothing is quite like the thrill of the chase to soothe the seeping wound. But the salve will lose its power, and the grief will return if it is not dealt with directly. Consider doing what a friend of mine calls "grieving well." Lean on friends for support, but be careful about early romances and living outside of your values sexually.

## The Road Is Hard

Scripture does not always promise an easy road. In fact, quite the opposite. Not only does Scripture talk about the challenges that will come into our lives, but the Christian life is even described as burdensome. We are told clearly that there will be tribulations. Yet we have an Overcomer on our side. (See Rom. 8:37; James 1:2–4.)

Christ spent most of his three years of teaching with a small group of disciples. Much of what he taught them involved loss, death, and sacrifice. Following Jesus was not an easy thing. A turning point in many of the disciples' lives occurred after Christ shared some particularly thorny truths with them: "I tell you the truth, unless you eat the flesh of the Son of Man and drink his blood, you have no life in you. Whoever eats my flesh and drinks my blood has eternal life, and I will raise him up at the last day" (John 6:53–54).

Christ was telling them that the flesh did not count for anything, that it was the Spirit that gave life. He was trying to get them to look beyond the physical aspects of his life and understand the concept of everlasting life. To lose your life was a small sacrifice to gain everlasting life.

Yet many disciples turned away from following Christ. He asked his twelve closest followers, "You do not want to leave too, do you?" (John 6:67). The apostle Peter said, "Lord, to whom shall we go? You have the words of eternal life. We believe and know that you are the Holy One of God" (John 6:68–69). In our more incisive moments, we echo the words of Peter. We want to run for dear life, but we too know that Christ has the words of life.

While many of Christ's teachings did not yet make sense to Peter, he had the wisdom to realize that in spite of all of the questions he had regarding the teachings of Christ, they far surpassed any knowledge he had about life. Though the road ahead would be daunting and the time in the crucible painful, it was the path to eternal life.

## Leaning into Change

Forcing ourselves to stay in the refining fire of the crucible means certain death. The heat is simply too much to bear. Yet it is that death that leads to transformation, and this time of brokenness is an opportunity to grow exponentially. It will require a delicate courage, but you can do it.

To lean into change sounds like an active process, but it actually can be an inactive process. It means staying put, right there in the ceramic container, amidst the blaze of red-hot emotions. It means letting yourself mull over what is happening, why it is happening, and what you are to learn from it.

Sue Monk Kidd describes this time well in her book *When the Heart Waits*. She says, "To create newness you have to cover the soul and let grace rise. You must come to the place where there's nothing to do but brood, as God brooded over the deep, and pray and be still and trust that the holiness that ferments the galaxies is working in you too. Only wait."[3]

So, against all natural inclinations to leap out of the crucible and off the treacherous path, the challenge is to sit still, wait, brood, and ponder. The writer of Ecclesiastes says,

"When times are good, be happy; but when times are bad, consider: God has made the one as well as the other" (Eccles. 7:14). During this time, you have much to consider.

To remain in the fire requires another crucial element not easily found. *It requires trust.* For many of us, trust can be as elusive as the wind. How can such a necessary component of change be so difficult to find and keep? What does this trust look like?

First, *trust implies a higher order to things beyond our rational minds.* Simply put, God is in control, and we are not. Trust says that we will let go of the tiller and let the winds of God fill our sails. Once we do this, we can let the tension in our grip soften. We are not the masters of this ship, in spite of our inclinations to the contrary.

Second, *trust recognizes a better way to do things, a way beyond our understanding.* Trust tells us that we will fare better if we let the Captain take the helm. We realize our fallibility and are humbled by it. Our lives have become unmanageable, and we need help from above to manage them.

Third, *trust recognizes that our fear must be confessed in order to be understood.* Perhaps we are afraid of being alone or that we will not get back with our mate. Perhaps we are afraid of having to ask for financial help. Any number of things may frighten us, but we must lean into them for change to occur. The antidote to much of our fear is the courage that comes from facing that fear.

Fourth, *trust requires action.* To simply say that we trust is no great feat. However, real trust demands that we put ourselves to the test. We step out in faith and face the fear of stepping beyond our safety net. We must be honest with ourselves about this issue of trust. If we trust, in whom do we trust? What new, trusting actions are required of us as we face our fears? Consider your current life situation: How do you need to step out in trust?

Finally, *trust is not an all or nothing proposition.* Many of us live in partial or incomplete trust. We make feeble attempts at letting go and then grab hold of the wheel again in order to recapture a semblance of security. We may feel like or say we have given up control of our lives but still be trying to hang onto it. The challenge, of course, is to practice trusting more completely.

## Summary

Growth rarely occurs without struggle. We see it in all forms of life—the seed pushing its way through the sandy soil; the mother and infant struggling during the birth process.

Our labor often requires grief, and even if we know it is good for us in the long run, we do not like to "grieve well." It is no fun to settle into the crucible with the refining fire. We all seek relief!

But remember that you have reason to be joyful, for the product of the fire creates cause for happiness and ultimate relief. Only after the dross has been sifted off can the glistening silver be seen. Here you can find the joy of discovery.

Consider how you have grown already in the time that you have been wrestling with your marital challenges. Consider the new gifts and strengths you now have to bring to your marriage. If reconciliation is not a possibility for you, acknowledge the gifts that you will take into your next stage of life or relationship. Refining fire produces a purity that is not obtained when things are going well. Though enduring the suffering is terribly difficult, thank God for his protective hand over you during these trying times. Thank him for the changes he is bringing forth in you even in this difficult moment.

# 10

## CONSIDERING RECONCILIATION

*Everything that I understand, I
understand only because I love.*

Leo Tolstoy

J ack had spent a lot of time in the crucible, a place of anxious and unsettled waiting. You recall that he had left his wife of seven years after feeling that the chasm between them could not possibly be bridged. He wrestled with his decision for months before deciding that he wanted more from a marriage. He had pled with his wife, Barbara, to spend more time at home with him and their children. But she was resolute in her desire to advance professionally and felt his demands were excessive. He had given up in despair.

I counseled Jack over the next year. I watched as he struggled, desperately trying to move forward with his life yet seemingly mired in quicksand. I watched as the left side of his brain rationally plotted out the course of his life and set his sights accordingly. I also watched as his right brain, the more emotional side, lost footing and settled into an enduring sadness. Letting go of his marriage was not as easy as he had planned or hoped. A cloud of memories hung over him as he wandered stoically forward.

Grief, as you well know, is a difficult enemy to dislodge. Some days are desperately gray; we take one step forward, two steps back. But because Jack spent time in the crucible, his turmoil was not all wasted. The refining fire was reshaping him. He spent more time in prayer and reflection than he had at any other time in his life, searching for a way to resolve his ambivalent feelings. Hardship and struggle are like magnifiers that bring priorities into pure focus. Jack's unrest was a sure signal that something needed more attention. Something needed to be changed. What was the hang-up? Why couldn't he let it go? Had he made the decision to move out too hurriedly? Had he not accurately counted the cost?

The cost. Jack had not been prepared for how much he would miss his family. He had not fully understood the price of so many hollow evenings in his apartment. He had not been prepared for the resurging feelings of missing Barbara, not to mention his children. The cost had been high, and he was paying the price. Jack's miscalculation was to believe that he could make a decision about marriage with as much detachment as he made decisions about money in the business world. He thought he could simply marshal his emotions and move forward expeditiously.

Although I did not meet with Barbara, I came to know her through Jack's description. At first he was not complimentary, but time softened his attitudes and perceptions. Now he described Barbara as a caring wife, albeit determined, preoccupied, and self-focused. I have no doubt that Jack's decision to end their marriage took its toll on her as well. Love lost and marital separation are momentous events in anyone's life.

Jack is every man; Barbara is every woman.

## Life on the Other Side

As Jack agonized over the loss of his marriage, he found himself wondering if it might somehow be possible to span the incredible gap between his wife and himself. He was not sure what she was thinking and did not know if she might be open to reconciliation. After all, she had made it perfectly clear that she wanted a lifestyle that was intolerable to him. How could their worlds be brought back together again? Was the rift too great to be bridged? While he was willing to consider compromises, he still wanted more time with his wife and family. Was God able to do what he and Barbara had been unable to do? Many questions nagged at him. He prayed for guidance and solace for his aching heart.

Like many couples in this situation, Barbara and Jack did not talk much—an occasional phone call to discuss difficulties with one of their children or a chance meeting at the local grocery store. Occasionally they still went to the same church, though Jack was exploring other possibilities as it was difficult seeing Barbara and answering questions from other church members. For the most part, their lives had already taken on new directions.

During his few conversations with Barbara, Jack learned that she was moving on with her life. While she had not wanted the separation and certainly had wanted to save their marriage, she had already begun to consider the possibility that divorce was inevitable. She had started to walk through the stages of letting go and had begun to embrace life as a single person.

Barbara was as practical as Jack. She was an astute businesswoman in her own right. She had earned a college degree and then established her own accounting firm. She had invested so much in her education and her career that she was not about to sacrifice it for what she felt was a "slim chance" of saving their marriage. She was cautious and concerned when she heard that Jack was reconsidering his position on their marriage.

The envelope came in the mail on a dreary fall afternoon. Barbara immediately recognized Jack's handwriting. She stacked the envelope with the bills she had received that day and decided to wait until she had made a cup of tea before opening it. She feared what might be inside; she had begun a new direction for her life and was not sure she wanted any communication with Jack.

She went to the kitchen and heated some water for tea. This was a rare day when she was able to be home before her children. As her children came into the house, she greeted them and asked about their day. Her thoughts, however, kept returning to the envelope. After several minutes she went back to the stack of mail, singling out the one from Jack. She was surprised at the flutter she felt as she looked at the envelope. She felt an odd mix of annoyance and encouragement. Would this be a friendly note, she wondered, or possibly another one of Jack's scoldings for the way she had handled some situation with the children?

She slowly opened the envelope. The card had a picture of autumn leaves in golds and browns with the words, "A Season of Hope." Inside the card, Jack had written a note.

"Barbara, it has been many months since we have been together. Seasons have come and gone, and time seems to have tamed a lot of the emotions I felt so long ago. I am surprised at how I feel today compared to how I felt six months ago. I am not sure what I want to say but would like to begin talking to you again. My heart is softer, and I wonder if you feel the same. I wonder if you have ever thought about a second chance at our relationship. Would you like to get together to talk? I would. I will call you in a few days to see if you would like to go out for a cup of coffee. A latte can cure a lot of ills. Love, Jack."

The children's voices were now a distant hum in the background. "Do I really want to open the relationship back up again?" Barbara wondered. "I have moved forward with my life. I have worked through a lot of things. Won't this just set me back? What exactly will he expect of me?" Her thoughts trailed off as she peered out the window to the lawn strewn with fallen leaves, much like the ones on the card. Was this, too, a sign that this was a new season, one of potential hope?

Barbara's questions mirror those that all couples facing this situation must ask themselves. Let's explore the issues together.

## Balancing the Equation

What does Barbara have to gain by considering reconciliation? What does she stand to lose? While it may sound detached and calculating to assess the issue in these terms, doing so will help us to truly understand the issues involved.

One of the first things that Barbara stands to lose by considering reconciliation is her chance to *play the victim.* Now this may not seem like much to give up, but many people seem to thoroughly enjoy playing the victim. Remember that Barbara did not want the separation. She did not fall out of love with Jack; he was the one who decided that he could not live with things the way they were. Jack questioned his feelings about her. Jack moved out. Subsequently, Barbara spent months nursing a grudge. While she was not willing to make the changes he sought, she had not asked him to leave. She had not asked for the separation. And since then she had rehearsed, many times over, how she had been wronged. She has found, as have many others, that luxuriating in righteous indignation can be strangely enjoyable.

Sidney and Suzanne Simon, in their book *Forgiveness: How to Make Peace with Your Past and Get On with Your Life,* say that giving up the victim position is one of the most important steps to reconciliation. They say that while you are trapped in your victim position, you radiate pain and misery. Because you are sending the same message over and over again, you stand no chance of things changing. "You have been acting out a victim script that has ended the same way every time and will continue to end that way," they write.[1] And so Barbara must first of all decide if she is ready to quit playing the victim and work through her resentment.

In considering reconciliation Barbara also stands to lose *independence*. She had been surprised at how nice it felt not to have to answer to Jack for many decisions. Especially near the end of their time together, she had felt hemmed in by his expectations and guilty for spending time at the office. Now she felt a sense of relief at only having to worry about pleasing herself and the children. As she thought about reconciliation, she wondered again what concessions she would have to make and whether she would be willing to make them.

When honest with herself, Barbara knew she still had a great deal of fondness for Jack, making his proposal tempting. As she reflected on the card, she wondered what it might be like to be happy together again. Could it possibly work? It would certainly be nice to be a happy family, as they had been in the past.

Perhaps the greatest obstacle to reconciliation is the psychological work involved. Barbara could imagine significant emotional wear and tear on both of them should they decide to move forward. Let's consider some of the stages they can expect to experience on the path back toward one another.

## Forgiveness and Reconciliation

Assuming that Jack and Barbara decide to move forward with reconciliation, many steps will be involved in the process. The first and perhaps most momentous is the issue of forgiveness. Both Jack and Barbara have wounds that will impede any efforts they make at reconciliation if they do not face them deliberately.

Before Jack sent the card, he spent countless hours in counseling pondering the possibility of reconciliation. He spent many hours venting his hurt and anger at what he perceived as his wife's betrayal. He also considered how he would need to let those feelings evaporate before he could offer an olive branch to her. She, in turn, needed to forgive him for walking out on her and their marriage. His actions seem contradictory to her—wanting more time as a family yet walking out on them. She still had some understandable tenderness about that issue.

Much of Jack and Barbara's preparatory work for reconciliation involved the issue of forgiveness. Much has been said and written about this thorny process. Frankly, a great deal of bad theology and psychology has been proffered on the topic. Forgiveness is not as easy or simple as many would lead us to believe, nor as impossible as others suggest. Faith can help us transcend our selfish nature, but forgiveness still involves a thorny process.

Dr. Tian Dayton offers a balanced perspective on the issue of forgiveness in her book *The Magic of Forgiveness*. The author outlines several stages of forgiveness. Note that she, like most other respected authors who talk about forgiveness, insists that it occurs in stages. *It is not an event but a process.*[2] However, as we consider these "stages," remember that forgiveness does not occur the same way for each person. Stages are also repeated during the healing process in many cases.

The first stage of forgiveness, according to Dr. Dayton, is *waking up.* She says that here we begin to see, as Jack did, that resentment and a desire for retribution cost us far more than they are worth. We begin to loosen our grip on the hostility we have harbored for so long. We begin to assess what it may be doing to us.

Not long ago I spoke to a middle-aged woman named Shelly who was going through the process of *waking up* as described by Dr. Dayton. She had silently held a grudge for a long time against her ex-husband, who had abandoned her. We discussed the various aspects of grief that she felt as she dealt with the rejection that ultimately led to their divorce. It had been a monstrous loss for her, and she had every right to feel enraged and rejected. But ever so slowly Shelly began to entertain the possibility that her anger was an impediment to healing. She was waking up.

The next stage, according to Dr. Dayton, is *anger.* She says that anger can be a productive emotion, because it often mobilizes us to necessary action. However, it can also lead to blaming and attacking one another, which is likely to cover feelings of vulnerability and perceived weakness. Giving up anger can feel like weakness, Dayton says, because we may feel like we are giving up some of our power. But the path of reconciliation involves an attitude shift, and being vulnerable comes with the territory.

The next stage is *hurt and sadness.* Dr. Dayton instructs us to embrace our grief, which has been a major theme in this book. She argues that failing to grieve sets us up for emotional and physical problems later. "When our trust and faith in a primary relationship has been shattered, we need to feel the pain and anger that shattering causes in us so that we can heal, move on and trust again," Dayton says. "Denied grief, anger and sadness ask future relationships to carry those powerful emotions that remain unfelt. Feelings from the past get displaced onto situations in the present. They get projected onto today's relationships—whether covertly or overtly—though their intensity may belong to yesterday."[3]

This is a most important truth: allow yesterday's emotion, sadness, grief, and loss, to be dealt with. Grieving allows us to separate our past from our present.

Jack had spent many hours recounting his story of rejection and loss. He cried hundreds of tears as he watched the demise of his family. Though far from innocent, he had never truly wanted the separation. He did, however, appropriately do much of his "grief work." By the time he considered reconciling with Barbara, he faced her with a fairly clean slate. The grudges he had held against her were gone because he had spent his time grieving. Gone was the rage and anger at being rejected, because he had spent his time examining the issue from different perspectives. He was no longer stuck being the victim; he was ready for a new day.

While I did not work with Barbara, Jack shared that she too had relinquished many hard feelings. She had spent time in the crucible as well, experiencing its refining fire. She too had let go of many of her hard feelings. However, she had to guard against comparing her path of healing to Jack's, for they were very different routes. She had to guard against letting others tell her where she "should" be on the healing path. The path of forgiveness is an intensely personal one.

The fourth stage of forgiveness includes *acceptance, integration, and letting go.* Dr. Dayton says that as we go through the process of getting past our carefully erected defenses and acknowledge the feelings below the surface, we may discover things about ourselves we had forgotten. Crises often crystallize what is important to us and result in moments of insight about ourselves. When we experience these epiphanies, acceptance does not seem as arduous as it did months or even just weeks ago.

In this stage of acceptance we often discover a new sensitivity toward ourselves and others. We are able to forgive ourselves for our failures; we are able to forgive our partners for their fragility and humanity. We begin to see that our spouse was probably doing the best they could under the circumstances. While they have done things that were very hurtful, we begin to see that we have done things that were equally hurtful and accept that we must take a portion of the blame.

Does acceptance mean that we forget the painful experiences? Certainly not. It simply means that we are no longer rehearsing what we perceive as the wrongs that were done to us. We have a looser grip on the painful issues of the past. *Letting go is a releasing of the past with an open hand.*

Christ gave powerful instruction on forgiveness: "Do not judge, or you too will be judged. For in the same way you judge others, you will be judged" (Matt. 7:1–2). These are sobering words. The verses following this recommend removing the log from your own eye before commenting on the speck in the eye of another. How we dislike those words! We easily see what others are doing wrong while retaining utter disdain for anyone who calls attention to our failures. Letting go requires the spiritual wisdom of knowing that it is time to move on.

Dr. Dayton says that the final stage of forgiveness is *reorganization and reinvestment.* "Having freed up energy that was weighing down our creativity and passion for living, we're able to reinvest that energy in satisfying life pursuits."[4] With this newfound energy, we are able to discern more accurately what we can and cannot expect of our partner. We begin to we see them more realistically and are not bound up in forcing them to behave in ways that are impossible for them. We give up control, or rather our feeble attempts at control. What a liberating experience! We have reached a stage where we have reasonable expectations of what we and our mate can bring to the marriage.

As you move through these stages of forgiveness, remember that the path is not linear. Rather, it is best thought of as a series of overlapping ellipses. We move forward, only to work on the same issues again from an advanced perspective. Just when we think we have dealt with an emotion or issue once and for all, it reappears. But this time we see it from a slightly different angle. Do not be disheartened when your anger resurfaces or you find yourself blaming your mate again for your troubles. Simply use it as another opportunity to do your emotional and spiritual work.

## A Broken and Contrite Heart

No progress can be made on the path of forgiveness and reconciliation without a broken and contrite heart. Scripture is clear about the importance of this. A broken heart is surely the seedbed for humility and a prerequisite for any reconciliation.

Consider what the life of David teaches us about brokenness. Here was a man of extremely humble beginnings who was destined to become a king. His epic tale gives average men and women hope that God can select anyone, even a lowly shepherd boy, to wield kingly powers. We cheer David on when he goes into battle wearing only a slingshot on his belt, the small shepherd boy facing the giant Goliath. It is a story of Hollywood proportions. Haven't we all felt that we were facing giants in our own land while armed only with a slingshot as a weapon? Certainly I have. In fact, many times I wished for as much as a slingshot!

But David's story proceeds along a path familiar to too many of us. A little success, some extra applause, the adoration of the crowd, and pride begins to creep in. Under such conditions we easily start to think we are better than the next person. We become inflicted with the disease of *entitlement*. Soon we become a bit haughty and judge others as less than ourselves. And the slide continues.

Like so many in our world today, as King David rises to stardom and power, he begins to think he can have it all. He demands to have whatever is pleasing to his eye, including the wife of another man. He has an affair with a lovely woman, Bathsheba, and purposely places her husband, Uriah, in harm's way. Uriah is killed in battle (see

2 Samuel 11). David has fallen a long way from our simple idol, playing his harp and singing psalms in the fields.

But as quickly as we are ready to be furious with King David for his gross sin, God sends a dose of heart-softener his way to remind him of what is right and what is wrong. Along comes the prophet Nathan, who tells David an allegory about a man who has everything yet takes from one who has nothing. Hearing the story, David is incensed that anyone would behave this way. How could anyone, in any situation, act with so much callousness and entitlement? Then, in one quick, incisive moment, the surgeon's knife finds the heart of the matter: David has done the same. David's defenses melt away with sadness and guilt as his actions are exposed. He immediately recognizes his shame, and with a broken and contrite heart is restored once again to the Lord's companionship (see 2 Samuel 12).

We must understand that we too are like David in every way, and we must find the strength to take ownership of our sins. Yes, the shepherd boy turned king teaches us that restoration and reconciliation are possible, no matter how far we have fallen. We see God swiftly and kindly bring a broken king to his senses. Though David had some residual pain from his actions—as we will—he could enjoy the presence and peace of God. What more can we ask for?

## Practical Steps of Reconciliation

You undoubtedly have walked a path strewn with stumbling blocks and potholes, and you undoubtedly have some bruises, as well as perhaps a wounded ego, to show for your journey. Thankfully, a bruised and broken heart is a wonderful place to begin the restoration of a relationship. From a broken heart we are teachable, humble, and willing to forgive. From a broken heart we empathize with others and feel genuine love. As you consider reconciliation with your mate after all that you have been through, a number of practical considerations will help you along the way.

Dr. Susan Heitler, in her book *The Power of Two,* shares tried and true direction for the lost and weary. Think about how you could apply her suggestions as you navigate through her list of practical tools for healing a broken relationship.[5]

First, she suggests that we *piece together the puzzle of what happened.* In this initial step you set aside your ego and your need to place blame and begin to reflect, non-judgmentally, on what has taken place. Here you are like a scientist, looking at the hard evidence, picking carefully between the different items to see what is relevant and what is extraneous. You assess what is your responsibility and what is not. Detective Friday of *Dragnet* knew what was really important when he said, "Just the facts, ma'am."

Stan and Ginger were preparing to reconcile after a lengthy separation. They had wisely agreed to come in for counseling to help them with the process. Initially, they found it very tempting to pin blame on one another. They had to be counseled repeatedly to set aside their emotions and remember the real purpose for meeting and talking about these issues: possible reconciliation.

"Every time I started to talk about how we had gotten to where we were, which was separated and facing divorce, I wanted to attack Ginger," Stan said. "I wanted to play the victim and make her out to be the bad guy. But that was not helpful, nor was it accurate. It was hard to steer clear of accusations and focus on the practical issues. I had to keep telling myself to let go of the anger. Let go of anything that was not going to help us come back together."

Ginger had her challenges too. "I wanted to get back with Stan, so it was more tempting for me to be quiet about the things that were really bothering me. But that wouldn't help us settle the problems that we still faced. I have always been one who would hold onto my anger and let it eat at me rather than being direct. I would find myself holding grudges and trying to get back at him by withholding my love and affection. I realized that these ways of getting even were just as damaging as an outright attack."

The second practical step discussed by Dr. Heitler is *apologizing*. This is such a fundamental step in healing. We all know that we must do this, yet my counseling experience tells me that people find it one of the hardest things to do.

I routinely ask couples with whom I am working whether it is easy for them to apologize. Almost without exception they tell me that *apology* is not in their vocabulary. I continue to be shocked by this response because I know that the words, "I am sorry; I was wrong," have the power to heal many conflicts. Yet for many reasons people have a hard time swallowing their pride and saying those humble words.

Dr. Wayne Dyer, in his book *There is a Spiritual Solution to Every Problem*, reminds us of the adage that three things are truly difficult to do in life: return love for hate; include the excluded; and say "I was wrong."[6] Oh, to have the heart

CONSIDERING RECONCILIATION

that Jesus taught in the Beatitudes—"Blessed are the poor in spirit. . . . Blessed are the pure in heart" (Matt. 5:3, 8)! He is speaking of those who are not so taken with themselves that they are unteachable. They are able to admit mistakes and learn from them. They have no need to appear perfect, for they know they are not.

Dr. Heitler's final and perhaps most powerful suggestion is *learn to convert the upset into shared growth*. We cannot say it too often: Every challenge is a chance for growth. Every time we face adversity, we also have an opportunity to emerge as a better self. The possibilities for growth and expansion are endless.

Listen to some final thoughts by Dr. Heitler: "If you react to an upset with anger, blaming your mate for the difficulty, you may actually feel more powerful, puffed up with righteous indignation. This feeling of larger-than-normal size brings a spurious sense of power, a power to control or hurt your mate, but does not necessarily give you the power to feel good about yourself. In contrast to the negative energy of angry power, true empowerment is not at your partner's expense. True empowerment does not depend on hurting your mate for you to feel good."[7]

**Pitfalls to Be Avoided**

With every fanciful dream of reconciliation comes the hard realities that must ultimately be faced. Gritty work must be done if the reconciliation is to be rooted in receptive ground. A number of pitfalls may waylay you on your journey toward reconciliation with your mate. The list includes

- holding onto judgments
- discouragement
- Pollyannaish thinking
- confusion
- distrust
- having excessively high expectations
- misunderstanding the feelings of your children
- having an unclear plan of action

Let's review them in more detail.

*Holding onto judgment.* Those who hold onto judgment see the world in distinctly black-and-white terms. Everything in their world is swathed in right and wrong, good and bad.

Kathy came to see me after being rejected by her husband of seven years, Paul. She had thought their relationship would remain strong forever. She did not anticipate his decision to separate and was devastated when he told her.

The separation process was horribly painful for Kathy. She was raw with emotion and found it difficult to eat or sleep for several weeks following Paul's announcement. But what hurt her the most was the sense of betrayal she felt. As if the separation were not enough to challenge her coping skills, she kept rehearsing how wrong his actions were.

When Kathy came to see me a few months later, I listened as she recounted the troubling news. While she told of the hurt and sadness that were overwhelming her, I was struck by how she had framed the situation. All she could tell me was how wrong Paul was in wanting the separation. She recounted how his actions were "sinful and against God's will." She insisted that he was the only one at fault in the situation and that she had done nothing to contribute to the conflict. I pressed her to look deeper, but Kathy clung tenaciously to the role of the victim and her belief that God would surely punish Paul for his actions. She felt entitled to her marriage and judged her husband for what he had done.

Obviously Kathy had a narrow perspective of the situation and would need to move beyond the limitations of right-and-wrong thinking to have any hope for emotional relief or reconciliation. She would need to give up the victim role and see things from a larger perspective. Only by acknowledging her part in the situation by rejecting the notion that Paul was exclusively "bad" could she create an opening for any fruitful discussion of their future.

Dr. Dyer says, "When we negotiate for peace, we generally see one side as wrong and the other as right. This is true in conflicts between nations, communities, families, and in your personal relationships too. You cannot bring spiritual harmony into a problem resolution as long as you accept the idea that one side is right and the other side is wrong. . . . Letting go of judgments concerning matters of right versus wrong, and simply finding a way of bringing nonjudgmental harmony to a problem, eliminates the ego's need to make someone wrong, which inevitably exacerbates the problem."[8]

*Discouragement.* Discouragement tells us that there is no hope, that things are never going to work out. It can be insidious, quiet, and very disarming. The voice of discouragement says:

- Things will never change.
- He/she will never change.
- You don't deserve anything better.
- Nothing works out the way I'd like.
- I must have done something to deserve this.
- I am the one at fault.
- He/she is the one at fault.
- I have no future if we don't reconcile.

When we get stuck in this mood, we are not processing things accurately. We believe the lies I listed above. We settle into right/wrong or good/bad thinking. We close ourselves off from the many possibilities that exist and from thinking from a larger perspective.

*Pollyannaish thinking.* This pitfall, often seen as the opposite of discouragement, is just as debilitating. In Pollyannaish thinking we believe that everything is going to work out easily. We survey the landscape and decide, incorrectly, that nothing out there can possibly throw us off course. This simplistic thinking does not adequately or accurately account for the size of the problem. It is like taking an aspirin to cure a brain tumor. Invasive surgery is needed, and anything short of that is a waste of energy. We must use wisdom to determine the size of the problem and our part in it. Then we can set about working on the solutions.

*Confusion.* When considering reconciliation, you need to be clear. This requires that you have taken time to reflect. You have considered the costs of reconciling, and you understand the benefits. While this may sound a bit crass, returning to your partner with significant ambivalence will do little good. Your mate will sense this immediately and will not feel safe with you. Confusion does not instill a sense of trust in the relationship, which is a necessary component of reconciliation.

*Distrust.* Every couple must create a safe environment where they are able to share their most vulnerable feelings. If betrayal has been an issue in your relationship, you undoubtedly have some repair work to do. You and your mate must work diligently at creating safety again. Generating this trust may take some time, but it can be done. Listen to Cynthia describe how she and her husband, Ty, created safety again.

"It was not easy to come back together after we had been apart for seven months. We had so much baggage between us. Ty was unfaithful in our marriage even before we decided to separate. He told me that he no longer loved me, and as soon as we separated he began seeing another woman. Now he tells me he wants to get back together. I'm not exactly rushing for the door to let him back in. He broke my heart, and I don't want to ever be hurt like that again."

I talked with Ty about his desire to get back with Cynthia. He understands that it will take a lot of work to create a safe, trusting space for them to share their love again.

"I know that I hurt her badly. I feel sorry for that and know that I was wrong. I am not asking her to trust me again right away. I know that if I prove myself, the love will grow back, slowly but surely. I can only hope that over time she will see that I am being genuine and truthful with her. I know that the secret is not to push her to trust me too soon."

Ty shows a lot of wisdom in his words. Many people push too fast for a show of support and trust. They do not realize that trust can be shattered in a moment and take years to grow again. But Ty also knows that it can be done, one step at a time.

*Having excessively high expectations.* While I do not want to be pessimistic, I do want to be realistic. In my clinical experience many who have tried to reconcile after love has been lost and trust broken meet challenges unlike any others they have previously confronted. Thus, they need to be ready for a very rocky path. While they need to move forward, they also need to be prepared for times of disappointment.

This is not meant to be discouraging. In fact, I am delighted when I hear that a couple wants to reconcile. Who cannot cheer when they see something that was broken being brought back to wholeness? It is truly wonderful.

So how do you manage your expectations?

- Acknowledge that reconciliation might take time.
- Understand that you may have disagreements.
- Know that old issues may surface again.
- Ready yourself for the fading of honeymoon feelings.
- Have a plan for counseling, if needed.

*Misunderstanding the feelings of your children.* If you have children, their thoughts and feelings about reconciliation will surely be important. In many cases they will be thrilled about you getting back with your mate. In some circumstances, however, children are less than thrilled at this prospect.

My caution to you here is that children deserve a voice in this decision. You may be asking your child to move back into a house that was once filled with tension. They may have significant distrust about doing so. Simply remember that the feelings and thoughts of your children should be considered. Should you fail to do so, their feelings will come out in passive-aggressive ways that will not serve them or you effectively.

The final pitfall is *having an unclear plan of action.* Reconciliation with your partner will likely be an arduous task. It will demand all of your emotional resources. You will need to be clearly focused on your goal in order to bring two disparate worlds back into harmony.

Your plan will need to include all of the issues discussed thus far in this chapter. You will need to deal with issues associated with the painful feelings in your past life as a couple; move ahead with a spirit of forgiveness; strengthen your abilities to communicate and deal effectively with conflict; have a heart ready to apologize and make necessary amends; and prepare for a course of reconciliation that may take more time and effort than you had originally hoped.

### A New Conversation

Jack and Barbara met for coffee. The first several minutes were as tenuous as a first date. Each wondered what the other was thinking and shared thoughts guardedly. Finally Barbara broke the tension by commenting that she felt like a teenager on a first date. Both grinned at their awkward situation.

After a positive first encounter, they agreed to meet again. They got together several times over the next few weeks and, as of this writing, are still seeing one another with the hope of reconciling. They have done many things right; they are following the steps offered in this chapter and being careful not to fall victim to the pitfalls common for couples in their situation. They have agreed to move forward cautiously, taking care not to rush things or have unreasonably high expectations. They are guardedly optimistic about their future.

Perhaps you are in similar circumstances. Perhaps you and your mate have begun a new conversation, or you are hopeful that it could happen. If you find yourself harboring the possibility of reconciliation, I suspect that if you don't take advantage of the opportunity, you will always wonder what would have happened. Even if things do not work out, you will know that you gave your marriage your best shot.

If you have already begun the reconciliation process and it is going well, you are quite fortunate. You know the obstacles that stood in the way of getting together again. You know the prayers that you have showered upon heaven to make this happen. Whether you were the one to leave or the one left, you know the chasm that had to be spanned for this to occur. Truly, it is time to rejoice.

While you may be understandably cautious, I encourage you to let love have its way. Stretch yourself to risk again. Could you be hurt? Of course. Are there any guarantees that it will work this time? Of course not. But should you find yourself with the opportunity and leaning toward trying it again, then by all means give it every chance. You risk a broken heart and a few bruises to your ego. But you stand to gain a renewed relationship with your mate and the restoration of your family. It's a chance worth taking.

## The Greatest Reconciliation Ever

In some ways, our struggle for a relationship with God parallels our relationship with our mate. We continue to drift from closeness to God, and yet mercifully we are given repeated chances to come back. Even after repeated separations, we are given continual opportunities to reestablish the relationship.

In the Genesis story of creation we read that humankind was given every possible luxury in order to live and thrive. But we squandered God's generosity. It was not enough to be given the Garden of Eden. We wanted more. Adam and Eve were not satisfied and were subsequently deceived by Satan. When Satan set forth the temptation, he knew the hearts of his prey were susceptible.

In the fall of Adam and Eve, we all took a giant tumble. Not only did we fall from innocence, but sin entered our lives for all time. No longer could we live in close communion with God, for God can have no part of sin. No longer could we enjoy the pleasures of Paradise.

Thankfully, the story does not end with humankind struggling beyond hope for renewed purity and reunion with the Father. It does not end with us being light years away from contact with God because of our sin. A bridge was built between us and God. A way was made back to Eden, and that same path may also be the way back to your mate. It is the path of humility and forgiveness. It is the path of recognizing our fallen nature and our need for a Redeemer.

We read in John 3:16 that Father God loved the world so much that he chose to sacrifice his Son, Jesus Christ, so that we could have everlasting life. Through that act of unimaginable love, the world can once again enjoy peace and fellowship with God. It is the greatest story of reconciliation ever told.

The power of that story should not be lost on us as we seek ways to heal a broken relationship and reestablish a union of love with our spouse.

## Summary

In this chapter you have learned that no matter how difficult or painful are the struggles we have encountered, reconciliation remains one of our most important challenges. It stands between our relationship to others, our relationship to God, and ultimately how we view ourselves. We can never truly be at peace until we have walked through the path of lost love.

# 11

# EMBRACING COMMUNITY, ENCOURAGING CHURCH

*Let us be grateful to people who make us happy; they are the charming gardeners who make our souls blossom.*

Marcel Proust

John trudged along the gravel path, head down, as the early mist still rose from the lake. He kicked rocks as he went, barely noticing as groups of joggers passed him. He felt as alone and as powerless as at any time in his life.

221

Several days earlier his wife, Carrie, had announced that she needed time to consider her lost feelings for him. She had taken their two young daughters and left to stay with her parents in a nearby city. His family, his life, all the props that kept him going were now gone. The house was unbearably silent this morning; he had to get out to keep his sanity. But nature provided little solace. He felt no more comfortable outside than he did in the eerie quiet of his home.

Carrie's departure had taken him by surprise, and he resented the power she now had over him. It was unfair, he muttered to himself. He'd invested so much in their marriage, and she'd taken it all away. Without Carrie and the children, his life was empty. His thoughts were riveted on one theme: How would he get them back? But there was another scenario that he tried not to consider: What kind of life would he have if they decided to stay away? How could he live without them?

When he came to a park bench, he sat down and watched elderly people feed the ducks. He watched smiling couples walk by, hand in hand. He listened as walkers discussed their lives. He peered into their worlds, feeling detached and distant.

## Going It Alone

Even if the situation is temporary, lost love and marital separation create the necessity of going it alone. While it may take months or years for the conflict to reach a flashpoint, when things finally fall apart, everything changes in an instant. Spouses can no longer rely on each other for comfort. They are no longer a team that faces and overcomes the tragedies that enter into every family's life. When a couple loses their commitment to each other, they often lose not only the solidarity they previously enjoyed but also the community they had been knitted into. The fabric of their lives is torn, often irreparably.

We have discussed the awkward position family members find themselves in when a couple wrestles with issues of commitment and possible separation. Friends and family, including the church family, are not sure how to react to the struggling couple. They are uncertain whether it would be best to comfort, encourage, or challenge the couple. Love lost is not an isolated affair; the ripples move out in every direction and last for a long time.

In response to their struggles, the couple often begins to act differently. As they struggle to define their new relationship, they commonly push away from their previous sources of support. This happens for several reasons.

First, *we often try to hide the guilt and shame we are feeling.* Those in a struggling and unhappy relationship often feel terrible about the tension in the marriage. When the struggle leads to a separation, both parties tend to feel a tremendous amount of shame for failing to make the marriage work, regardless of who does the leaving. In our culture and particularly in the Christian subculture, a stable marriage seems to be almost a prerequisite for church membership. People in churches have a tendency to look good, act good, and attempt to be good. Having a faltering marriage is not in the equation for many churches, so when a couple is separating, they often push away rather than have their "dirty laundry" viewed by others.

Second, *we fear rejection.* Having already experienced rejection from your spouse, you are probably unwilling to be rejected again, especially by people who cannot or will not understand what you are experiencing. You are in no mood for lectures or clichés. In fact, your tolerance level for anything approaching criticism may be at an all-time low. Because you are raw with emotion, any perceived criticism could feel intolerable. So to protect yourself, you withdraw; it is a perfectly natural tendency.

Third, *the conflict absorbs a tremendous amount of psychological energy.* Let's face it—when love is lost and commitment is questioned, some degree of conflict has led up to this action. All of these battles, including preparing for a possible separation, take energy to resolve. You may notice that you feel less energetic and enthusiastic and more tired and emotionally absorbed in the struggle. Not only do you need to pull away in order to deal with these issues, but you probably do not wish to talk about them publicly. You need time to pull in, create a safe nest, and reflect upon what is happening. Your damaged emotions require a rest from unnecessary questions.

Finally, *we fear being vulnerable.* Again, letting others into the inner sanctuary of your life can be difficult. You may be accustomed to "being strong" and handling things on your own. Work, responsibilities, children, and household chores all add up to create layers between you, your feelings, and others. When some of those layers are stripped away, you may suddenly feel frighteningly vulnerable. You are more in touch with feelings and thoughts that had formerly been hidden away under the veneer of propriety.

## Pamela's Story

Pamela is a forty-one-year-old woman who came in for counseling after years of "emotional disconnection" from her husband, Paul. She agonized over her feelings, or lack of them, for many months prior to her first appointment. She had kept her feelings silent, never sure what her next step should be. She gradually shared her story of a long-term relationship held together by the hope that things would somehow improve. I watched the sadness fill her eyes as she spoke.

Pamela told me that she saw hints of infidelity, though no signs so blatant as to give her justification for leaving Paul. She wondered why else he would be so distant and detached from her. For years she harbored feelings of disenchantment and loss and now threatened Paul that if he did not attend therapy with her soon, their marriage would be in more serious trouble. In his maddeningly stoic way, he informed her that he had no intention of attending counseling. He told her that he had been this way when she married him and was not about to change now. He pointed out that he had done nothing wrong in their marriage to warrant her leaving. Pamela thought more about the possibility of taking a "breather" from him to reflect upon her feelings.

As she talked about her plans for a future without Paul, she was surprised to find that a number of obstacles prevented her from exploring her feelings. Her community, which was comprised primarily of her family, her longtime church friends, and her co-workers, frowned upon her leaving Paul just so that she could "explore" her feelings. Church friends and family had seen the dangers of separation—too often, divorce was the inevitable outcome. Many people voiced concerns about her actions; they offered little in the way of encouragement. She found out quickly enough that what she was proposing was not in keeping with her church's beliefs.

> *No man is an island entirely of itself; every man is a piece of the continent, a part of the main.*
>
> John Donne

What made matters worse was that Paul had gone to their pastor and complained about Pamela's failure to support his marital authority. The pastor had apparently told Paul that leaving the marriage, even briefly, was never a viable option. Shortly after Paul won over the pastor, Pamela was confronted about her pending decision. She resented this but pushed her feelings aside, at least temporarily. Slowly, however, she felt rejected by her community and withdrew from it.

"I feel like people don't understand what I'm going through," she said. "People are quick to give advice, and they mean well, but they don't get it. They haven't walked in my shoes and can't give me advice that fits my situation. I guess I set myself up for it though, because I asked for their input. But it doesn't feel good to be considering separation and have so few people tell me they support me. They don't know that I have lived for years without love in my life. I can't continue like this any longer. I have to get some distance to evaluate what is best for me and my marriage. Maybe a little space will cause Paul to think things over too."

Pamela felt keenly disappointed in her community. She had to search for supportive people, as do many in her situation. Finding support is often a process. People often feel abandoned by their community, and they do not realize how important that support has been to them until they are without it. They realize that without the safety of the larger body of friends and family, they are both alone and isolated. Imagine adding these feelings to those associated with leaving your spouse and you can easily understand why people feel overwhelmed.

## The Importance of Community

Losing the love of your mate is difficult. It is challenging to your physical health, your emotional well-being, and your spiritual vigor. The troubles that accompany lost love can drain the energy out of you, and you must consciously replace it. One of the refueling stops on this journey is *community*.

I have a close friend who repeatedly admonishes me to make sure that I keep the legs to my stool of community intact. "Have you called your friends this week?" he chides me. "Why has it been so long since you've reached out to me?" He reminds me that if I don't cultivate my support community, it will not be there when I need it. His words always cause me to pause and reflect upon my life: How am I doing at keeping my community of support intact?

> *Do not forsake your friend and the friend of your father, and do not go to your brother's house when disaster strikes you—better a neighbor nearby than a brother far away.*
>
> Proverbs 27:10

Community is something larger than your close personal friends. It includes them, of course, but is more than that. It also includes your neighbors, your work associates, those with whom you worship, and perhaps even acquaintances. In a way it can also include people in your city that you recognize but have never spoken to. Community is a large network of people that you feel some connection to, no matter how minor. It has the power to be a creative and positive force in our lives, to be neutral, or even to be negative and draining for us.

Reflect for a moment on the people who comprise your community. Consider their value and their importance to you. What role will you allow them to play in your life, especially during a challenging time?

Mitch Albom, in his popular book *Tuesdays with Morrie*, tells of his moving experience with community. The story takes place in a nursing home where a professor from years earlier is dying from Lou Gehrig's disease. Blessed with an extra measure of humanity and an incredible ability to relate to others, Mitch walks the daily death march with his aging professor, Morrie, through his last days on Earth. Mitch cares enough that he doesn't turn away from death. He and Morrie create a mutually gratifying experience because of their friendship throughout this adversity.

At one point near the professor's death, Morrie asks his former student, "Mitch, all this talk we're doing. Do you ever hear my voice sometimes when you are back home? When you are all alone? Maybe on the plane? Maybe in your car?"

"Yes," I [Mitch] admitted.

"Then you will not forget me after I'm gone. Think of my voice and I'll be there."[1]

Morrie and Mitch's story shows us the importance of personal community—that we need to be available to one another throughout every aspect of life.

## Rejecting Community

Community has a powerful influence in our lives, perhaps more than we admit. In many ways it shapes how we think, behave, and respond to life's circumstances. Most of us want the approval of the larger community; most of the time we can get it. But sometimes we can't, and that can be particularly troubling.

Through our support community, we realize that we are "all in this together." We need love from others; they need love from us. In her book *The Art of the Possible*, Alexandra Stoddard says, "Just as a parent continues to love and care for a child even after the child has grown up and become physically and emotionally independent, so must we offer support and encouragement to others even when they cannot respond in kind."[2]

Unfortunately, communities too often fail by offering neither support nor neutrality. Instead, they offer criticism and rejection. Even in the community we trust in times of need, we will inevitably find those who fail to respond with kindness to those that are hurting. This behavior is, in many ways, unconscionable. A community has an obligation to support its members since we are all intricately knitted together, for better and for worse.

Kelly shared with me the story of how she fared during her recent separation. Her friends, all of whom were married, looked down on her. Their response was not blatantly offensive, but, she said tearfully, "I could feel it." She realized that in her friends' minds, separation was not an acceptable action. When it occurred, someone obviously deserved the blame. Sensing their underlying criticism, Kelly felt backed into a corner. She tried to defend herself, feeling shamed by their rejection and lack of support, but to no avail. While her friends politely echoed what sounded like understanding, she felt that they neither understood her nor were sincere in offering support. She was forced to move forward alone and depressed.

## The V Formation

At times in your marital struggles you may wish to withdraw from your community. I don't think you truly want to be alone but rather don't have the strength to ask for the help you need. You don't have the energy to put on a happy face, and being a part of the group simply requires too much effort.

Geese know how to live in community. They fly in their characteristic "V" formation because it decreases wind resistance. The ones in the back don't have to work as hard because the ones in front are breaking the wind for them. The leader takes the greatest resistance, so the geese take turns leading.

Geese also know how to take care of their own. When one of the flock is too tired or ill to keep up with the rest, another will fall back with it until it recuperates enough to rejoin its flock or connect with another one.

These birds know something that we need to practice. They live, breathe, and exist in community. They do not let one of their own fall by the wayside. They are on the journey together.

Effective communities are places where burdens can be shared, easing the load for everyone. Galatians 6:2–5 provides a wonderful lesson on sharing another's burdens:

> Carry each other's burdens, and in this way you will fulfill the law of Christ. If anyone thinks he is something when he is nothing, he deceives himself. Each one should test his own actions. Then he can take pride in himself, without comparing himself to somebody else, for each one should carry his own load.

We are admonished to carry each other's burdens. When we do this we fulfill the law of Christ. The Greek word for *burdens* here means *excess burdens*—that is, the issues of life that are simply too difficult for us to handle alone. While we may attempt to heroically plod through a crisis alone, it was not meant to be that way in God's economy. When burdens are excessive, *we need the support of a caring community.*

A verse later we are told to carry our own load. This might seem to be contradictory advice, but it is not. Here the Greek word for *load* is *the burden of daily toil.*[3] We are expected to "carry our share of the load," in other words.

A healthy community encourages its participants to do their part, as they are able, in assisting those with burdens that are too heavy to carry alone. These words urge us to look squarely in the mirror. We must determine which burdens we can carry and which will require help. Many times the anguish of separation will be far too great to carry alone. When that occurs, you would be irresponsible *not* to reach out for help.

As you reflect on the topic of community, ask yourself if you have developed an adequate support network of friends and family as well as a larger sense of community among neighbors, co-workers, and acquaintances. Do you have someone you can call on at any time of the day or night for help if necessary? Do you feel connected to your larger community? If not, you can still begin the task of finding a support group, be it a church or activity group where you can cultivate friendships. You may want to consider volunteering, even at this difficult time in your life, to help you feel as though you are part of the larger community. Keep the legs of your stool strong and in place.

**The Power of Community**

On fateful September 11, 2001, I was in southern Italy with my son. We passed a pub where a group of Italian, British, and American people was riveted to CNN. When my son and I entered the pub and moved close to the monitor, we saw what most Americans now have indelibly imprinted in their minds: the constant replaying of jetliners exploding into the twin towers; people running for their lives in terror; the president addressing the nation in an effort to create solidarity and stave off panic. Perhaps most importantly, we witnessed a larger sense of community that extended beyond the Americans in the pub. Our hearts went out to those in New York and Washington, D.C., and we provided assistance by sending money and prayers.

My son and I felt strangely disconnected from our homeland. Although we could not have done anything to help, we felt a need to be at home with our family as they grieved and feared for the safety of our nation. We felt a far-reaching sense of community. We cared what was happening to fellow Americans.

Campaigns to care for one another, to assist in carrying each other's burdens, were in the forefront of everyone's mind. National pride rebounded, as it often does during times of crisis. In smaller ways, family and community pride rebounded in the face of tragedy. When the chips are down, we go to bat for one another, as we should.

Today the chips may be down for you. Today may be a difficult time for your marriage. Conversely, this can be a wonderful time to increase solidarity with your family and friends. It is a time to let others rally behind you and care for you. Can you let them do it? While it may take time, and being critically selective, there are people ready to care for you.

### Koinonia

Of greater importance than national pride and solidarity is the community of Christian believers. Long before we came to appreciate the value and power of community, God created us to live in relationship to one another. He created a community where individuals would be part of something that was organic, growing.

*Koinonia* is a Greek term with a variety of meanings, including *community, participation,* and *communion*. It refers to a gathering of believers for the purpose of sharing what they have in common, from resources to ruin. The Scripture commonly cited to describe *koinonia* is Acts 2:42–46. It reads:

> They devoted themselves to the apostles' teaching and to the fellowship, to the breaking of bread and to prayer. Everyone was filled with awe, and many wonders and miraculous signs were done by the apostles. All the believers were together and had everything in common. Selling their possessions and goods, they gave to anyone as he had need. . . . They broke bread in their homes and ate together with glad and sincere hearts, praising God and enjoying the favor of all people.

Imagine being supported and loved within such a community where everyone gives to one another "as he had need." But notice that the focus for this group was their faith, out of which they praised God continually and thus had "glad and sincere hearts." Community has power, and we can take parts of this model and apply them to our lives.

Paul Escamilla, in discussing this passage and the phenomenon of *koinonia,* says,

> We know such closeness with God and those around us when we harmonize a hymn, share the bread and cup, take each other's hand in passing the peace or saying hello, wink at a child peering over the next pew, speak our prayers of confession, wait together in silence, come to the altar rail for prayer or healing, receive a word of blessing. As we

share with others in the worship of God, we become intimately bound up with God and one another in more ways than we know.[4]

*Koinonia*—a community of believers sharing all they have, from hurts to hopes. Certainly you who are in the throes of marital separation can use a little comfort from the larger community. As they say in the Alcoholics Anonymous tradition, in the group there is experience, strength, and hope available for all. Where can you find this kind of true community?

> *Two are better than one,*
> *because they have a good return for their work:*
> *If one falls down, his friend can help him up.*
> *But pity the man who falls and has no one to help him up!*
>
> Ecclesiastes 4:9–10

## The Imperfect Church

Sadly, some communities of believers are not only imperfect but unsafe as well. I have talked to many who have experienced one or more of these communities. Tragically, too many have found that the place they expected to find sanctuary from life's greatest stressors was the most unsafe.

The central element of an unsafe church is *shame*. The very people we need and expect to embrace us can, and sometimes do, treat others in a way that defies Christ's teachings. No one can be perfect. The church that implies that it is important to be perfect, to look good, sets the Christian up to fail. It is important that the church makes it safe to be "real" as we strive to be godly people. We all need to understand the face of shame and how to guard against this damaging kind of community.

Shame is the feeling that *who we are,* as opposed to what we have *done,* is wrong. Our very personhood is inadequate in some way. We are told that we could become "right" if we just followed certain steps outlined for us. But the bottom line is that we are wrong to be where we are or to feel what we feel.

John Bradshaw says in his groundbreaking work *Healing the Shame That Binds,* "Worth is measured on the outside, never on the inside. . . . Toxic shame is about being flawed as a human being. Repair seems foreclosed since no change is really possible. In its ultimate essence, toxic shame has the sense of hopelessness."[5]

Ron and Vicki Burks, in the book *Damaged Disciples,* tell the story of belonging to a church movement that sapped their very life and attacked their unique personalities. This church directed their behavior rather than focusing on the cross and a relationship to Christ. In the process of trying to do good, feel good, be good, and act good, they not only lost the vibrancy of their faith but felt a deep sense of abiding shame and inadequacy.[6]

Consider whether or not you have fallen into a road to perfection, one of the major root causes of shame, as outlined in *Healing for Damaged Emotions* by Dr. David Seamands:

- Tyranny of the "oughts": an overall feeling of never doing well enough or being good enough;
- Self-depreciation: you may never be satisfied with yourself and your achievements;
- Anxiety: the "oughts" and self-depreciation produce an over-sensitive conscience under a giant umbrella of guilt and shame;
- Legalism: you may demand that you adhere to a rigid emphasis on externals, a list of do's and don'ts;
- Anger: there is a resentment about the list of "shoulds" and "oughts";
- Denial: often the anger is not faced, but rather denied, with accompanying mood changes.[7]

A quick review of this list may convince you, as it does many people, that you have fallen short of the perfectionistic standard set by many churches and succumbed to the debilitating effect of shame. Fortunately, that is not the end of the story. You can begin to rebuild your life with a healthier set of guidelines. You can find and to a certain extent create a healthy community that surrounds you with acceptance rather than shame.

## An Embracing Church

Thankfully, many churches do meet our need for fellowship *and* acceptance. I have found in recent years that more churches are reaching out to the walking wounded—that is, you and me—and offering them a cool drink from the gospel of grace. In such instances people come to their senses, take

off their pious robes, and greet one another with a warm and
hearty embrace regardless of race, financial status, marital
situation, or emotional well-being. Instead of a suspicious
look of scorn and shame, we receive one another with the
acknowledgment that we have been in their shoes at some
time and know they need a big hug and a word of encouragement, not a lecture or a glare.

In his book *The Ragamuffin Gospel,* Brennan Manning
offers a radical perspective that may take some reflection to
fully appreciate. He writes, "The gospel of grace announces:
forgiveness precedes repentance. The sinner is accepted
before he pleads for mercy. It is already granted. He need
only receive it. Total amnesty. Gratuitous pardon."[8]

Who cannot relate to the rebellious son or daughter who
longs to come back home? Who of us is not warmed and
encouraged by the parable of the prodigal son (see Luke
15:11–32)? You remember that the youth took his inheritance and spent it on wine, women, and song. Destitute,
he came crawling back. We are surprised and encouraged
by what happens next. The Scriptures tell us, "But while he
was still a long way off, his father saw him and was filled
with compassion for him; he ran to his son, threw his arms
around him and kissed him" (Luke 15:20).

The father does not give his son a tongue-lashing and
demand a detailed explanation of his actions. Rather, he
gives what we all want and need: a warm and loving embrace
that cries out, "I have missed you so! I am glad you are safe
now and that you have found your way back home. Let's
celebrate as a family."

Now what if we, as a body of believers, could carry
that attitude to those around us? What if, when someone

was "a long way off" emotionally, spiritually, or physically, we grabbed them, flung our arms around them, and said we loved them? What if we would not let them pull away?

I have been blessed with some very special friends. All of them have done wonderful things for me at different stages of my life. One friend, Jack, has reached out to me again and again during some tough times when I was tempted to pull away. He has never been overly forceful, but he always encourages me to remain a part of the larger community, regardless of my circumstances. His genuine affection and tenacity have impacted me deeply.

Perhaps you have experienced both the harmful church community and the healing church community, as I have. The unhealthy, shaming community caused great pain for me. Now I am part of a healing community of believers. The healthy, healing community says to me and to you:

- You are accepted where you are, as a fellow seeker.
- You do not need to clean up before showing up.
- You have something to offer.
- Your past does not matter today.
- You are loved.

If this book finds you in a dry spiritual place, perhaps as a result of being spiritually wounded, I hope that you will reach out again and find a church, and healing community, that offers the comfort and acceptance you need.

## The Helping Church

Thankfully, many churches are sensitive to hurting, separated, lonely people who are experiencing lost love. They are attuned to their needs and want to be relevant in their faith walk. They take seriously the Scripture that tells us, "If one of you says to him, 'Go, I wish you well; keep warm and well fed,' but does nothing about his physical needs, what good is it?" (James 2:16). These churches know that one of the surest ways to touch people's hearts is to help them in their greatest hour of need.

However, we, the church, must do more than wish one another well. We must reach out to you who are suffering the pain of marital separation. What are some considerations for us, the church?

First, *the church is perfectly equipped to meet many of the needs of those suffering from lost love.* Why do I say this? Because you have already been a part of the church community, care about that community, and are cared about in return. Just as the biological family stands up for members when they are down, so too the spiritual family can stand up for those within it who are down. An established bond, a sacred trust that has been developed over time, already exists. Relationships have been developed in Sunday school classes, in the choir, at marriage retreats. This family has built *trust.*

Second, *the church community has many of the resources needed for healing:*

- safety
- understanding
- wise counsel

- biblical encouragement
- friendship
- structure

The church family has many resources at its disposal and can offer them freely to you, either individually or as a body. The church is comprised of members who have gifts of money, housing, and practical skills. Perhaps every need will not be met, but a great deal can be given to you.

Third, *the church community is designed by God to meet these kinds of needs.* We have already illustrated the scriptural mandate (Gal. 6:2–5) to care for one another by meeting needs. Not only are we doing what is required of us, but by doing so we are blessed and fulfilling the biblical directives.

Finally, *the church community will become more cohesive in the process.* Consider how a friendship is strengthened as the individuals stretch and grow together. Adversity seems to strengthen bonds between individuals and families. Remember that we are all one body, "and each member belongs to all the others" (Rom. 12:5).

## Our Need to Belong

Within each of us is the desire to belong, to be understood. Life can leave us so lonely. Anyone who experiences a traumatic event such as separation tends to automatically feel separated from others. Everyone around us appears to be married, happy, and unimpressed with our plight.

Right now you do not feel a part of the larger whole. In one fell swoop, you have become disengaged from the community. Such is the natural feeling of grief and loss. "No one understands," you say. "No one cares. I am alone with this problem."

If you are dealing with lost love, now more than ever you need a faithful friend and *a faithful community*. You need to belong; you need a sense that you are important and that others will walk you through this calamity and nurse you back to health. In the community of faith, people know what you are going through and care enough to remember the things you are confronting: that this is the day that you will be meeting your spouse for marriage counseling, or that you will be going in for that job interview. They know that these days are filled with uncertainty and you need an extra dose of TLC.

We all have a need for community. But community will not come to you automatically. You will need to reach out and look for ways and places that you can belong. It would be nice if people would just sense our need and come running after us. But that is not going to happen. It is up to you and God. When you are ready and ask God for special friendships and community, he will show you the way. Be prepared for action. Be prepared to take risks by reaching out to others and asking for help. Set aside any excess of pride or timidity.

## Summary

We all need to belong. When life is going well, friends make life even more joyful. When things are not going well, friends and community become an absolute necessity. The Scriptures are written in the context of community—repeatedly we are told to be reconciled to one another, to support one another, and to encourage one another. Certainly when experiencing love lost, you need the love and prayers of family and friends more than ever.

Our final chapter will talk even more about how to find new ways of moving beyond this difficult time in your life.

# 12

## NEW MOORINGS

*One of the pleasantest things in the
world is the journey.*

William Hazlitt

Jackie slowly sipped her coffee as she pored over the morning paper. One ad in particular jumped off the page: "Nicely furnished two-bedroom apartment in the West Hills area. Close to parks and schools. Pets OK. Won't last. Call 555-0267." She took a deep breath, scanning the ad again for additional clues. She could imagine the setting and knew it would work perfectly for her. It seemed too good to be true. She paused and silently breathed a quick prayer.

Newly separated, terribly alone, and frightened about her future, Jackie focused on taking one simple step after another. As she reached for the phone and dialed the number, she prayed, "God, if this is what you want for me, let it be available. If not, I leave my future in your hands."

She needed a place to recover from the announcement her husband, Daniel, had made two months ago—that he was no longer in love with her after their seven years of marriage. She wanted to feel safe and hoped she would not be forced to settle for an apartment complex where she would be hearing sirens at all hours of the night. She needed this apartment.

The last two months had felt very long. She had felt like her world was crashing in around her. She had never had such a loss. Her world had always been safe, protected. Her parents were still together after twenty-seven years and in fact still lived in the same house on a tree-lined street in a sleepy town in Wisconsin. She hadn't yet told them about her marital struggles. She and Daniel had yet to decide what exactly was to happen between them, since he was uncertain about what he wanted to happen with their relationship.

Jackie hated the loose ends of her life. While she wanted their marriage to work, she did not like waiting for Daniel to make a decision about it. She wondered about telling him that if he needed time to decide, he could have all the time he wanted while she filed for divorce. But she did not really want a divorce, so she tried to settle into a time of waiting—waiting for him to think about their marriage, family, and life together. It was an anxious time for her.

Jackie fidgeted with the phone cord as she listened to the ringing of the phone. A friendly voice answered, and Jackie asked if the townhouse was still available. It was. She gave the woman a summary of her circumstances, how she was planning on living alone for several months to consider the direction of her life. She offered more information than necessary, but lately she'd found that her life story seemed to slip out before she could catch herself.

The woman voiced some concern about Jackie's situation, especially her ability to pay. After some reassurance, the woman invited Jackie over to look at the place, talk with her, and, provided things went well, fill out a rental agreement. Jackie sighed a prayer of thanksgiving as she hung up the phone.

Jackie was offered the apartment, and she quickly accepted. She knew that this was a place where she could weather the storm of her life. In the following weeks Jackie moved some of her things and those of their three-year-old son, Timothy, from the house they'd shared with Daniel for seven years to their new home. Although it was a foreign place and she was frightened about being alone, she felt a curious sense of peace. She hoped the apartment would be a place to help her develop a new sense of direction for her life. She was beginning the process of setting up new moorings that would provide stability in her tempestuous circumstances.

## A Need for Anchors

Amidst the emotions that accompany lost love and separation—from abject panic to the bewildering state of confusion—everyone needs anchors. We need to be able to take refuge from the storm in a safe harbor.

As a sailor, I am keenly aware of the value of a good anchor. The best bury themselves into the sand and hold fast to the ocean floor. Winds and waves cannot pry them loose. Those that are less effective will pull loose under the pressure of a sudden gust of wind. When the winds are too stiff and the harbor is too far away, I am grateful to have an anchor that will hold. Then, when all is secure, I pour myself a cup of coffee and remind myself that I must simply practice patience. I must trust in my preparation and my anchor. And this is precisely what you must do as you face this time of uncertainty.

When everything in your life feels unsettled and you are unsure of what tomorrow will bring, what anchors can be helpful? How do you find those that will provide adequate stability?

You need to *simply find a safe haven away from the stormy emotions of lost love.* When we are experiencing a crisis, our thoughts focus on that crisis, and this gives way to panic and confusion. You may tend to think about the troubling situation over and over again. Try as you might, you can't get the problem out of your mind. The challenge is to find that safe harbor where you can let the panic drift away, leaving you with a mind capable of clarity and vision. But how is this accomplished?

First, *you can create stability in your external world.* Although there were many things Jackie could not control, she knew that having a home that belonged solely to her would be helpful. She also wanted a place where she could have her cat, her plants, and enough room to focus her energies on her son. She knew that he would require more time and attention because of the separation from his father.

Jackie had collected and cultivated plants for years. She now surrounded herself with them, and they gave her delight and a sense of emotional stability at the end of a day at the office. Her plants, along with Timothy, distracted her from the pain of waiting for Daniel to decide about his feelings toward her. Here in her own apartment she could create a world that was predictable and stable, unlike the rest of her world which had come crashing down on her.

Jackie was careful to pick an apartment in a nice section of town that would be free from crime and noise. Knowing that her emotions would be volatile and she would be prone to overreaction, she wanted to feel completely at ease. She chose a place that was close to a popular park where she could take Timothy to play outside and walk in at night in safety. She knew that her friends would feel comfortable visiting her new place.

Second, *you can surround yourself with things that are nurturing to you.* Jackie immediately purchased some new lighting for her townhouse. She knew that during the winter months it would take extra effort to make the townhouse look bright and inviting.

Jackie invited her friends over to help give the rooms a fresh coat of paint. She needed colors that reflected her personality and chose a blue to offer a sense of energy, yellow to reflect sunlight on even the darkest days, and browns that seemed to give her comfort. This was going to be her place to grieve and grow. The space needed to provide opportunity for her to do that work.

For the first several weeks, she found herself listening to romantic music that she had enjoyed with Daniel. She soon noticed, however, that it only discouraged her and

reminded her of the lost love in her life. She purchased a
mix of new music, including some Christian music, and
found it very uplifting.

Jackie also carefully selected books that had been recommended to her to help her through this crisis. She had
several different types of books for different purposes. She
purchased books dealing with marital separation but especially enjoyed the books dealing with transitions. She felt
like she was facing the biggest transition of her life. She also
had a daily devotional to help get her day off to a positive
start. The devotional reminded her that although her outer
world was unmanageable, her inner world could be peace-
ful. She clung to verses that assured her of God's comfort
and concern for her situation: "Peace I leave with you; my
peace I give you. . . . Do not let your hearts be troubled and
do not be afraid" (John 14:27); "in all things God works for
the good of those who love him" (Rom. 8:28).

Third, *friendships provide an anchor of stability in difficult
times.* Consider your friendships, old and new. Who will
offer you comfort and peace in this unsteady time? Can you
cultivate any new friends to add to those who have been
there for you in the past?

Jackie was determined to make this separation a time to
rebuild her friendships. While at times she felt like a burden,
she tried to move beyond those feelings and simply enjoy
her friends. They arranged fun things to do—some with
their children, some without. They went to some parks and
trails near the city she hadn't explored before. They agreed
to visit one new, inexpensive restaurant every week. They
would occasionally see a play in a neighboring city. Through

these friendships and activities, Jackie began rediscovering parts of herself she had left behind.

While you may lose some friendships during this difficult time, you can gain new ones if you set out to do so. You will not be left unsupported. Your life is changing, and you should not let yourself focus solely on your losses. Look to the new people who are entering your life. What dimension are they adding that you would not have had without this crisis?

Fourth, *you can create a positive attitude which finds a sense of purpose and intention in all that is happening in your life.* This usually does not come easily. You must develop an ability to find the dark cloud's silver lining. How has this separation affected you? What new things has it taught you about yourself and your marriage? Have you learned to "lean into" your struggles and emerge stronger on the other side?

Consider the lessons you have learned already. Perhaps you have discovered that you are too possessive of your mate. Perhaps you have realized that you need to control your tongue or that you need to be more generous in giving praise and affirmation. Perhaps you have found that you need to be kinder and more loving to yourself. The lessons can be endless. Do your best to think of this difficult season as preparation for a new day in the life of your relationship with your partner or a life alone for a while.

Alexandra Stoddard, author of *Gracious Living in a New World,* tells of a challenging period in her life when she chose to create quiet time for reflecting and creating a clearer purpose. "I felt a spiritual transformation and vitality I had never known before. I was able to relax enough, to remain quiet long enough, to allow deeper observations and reflections to rise up in me. I took time every step of the way. . . . Only in solitude are we able to daydream."[1]

Jackie set aside a few minutes each morning to define how she wanted this separation to change her. Rather than being a "victim of circumstance," she wanted to develop a positive attitude and make it a productive time. So she examined her circumstances for growth possibilities. "How can this time apart from my husband be good for me?" she mused. "How can this time of low income be good for me? What are the gifts in this time apart?"

> *O Lord, you are so good to the soul who seeks you. What must you be to the one who finds you?*
>
> Bernard of Clairvaux

Fifth, *remember that this new place you are in has the power to make you a deeper and richer person.* You may find yourself alone in an apartment for the first time in your life. You may be in a new city that challenges you to learn to make friends. You may be in a new church that requires adjusting to new surroundings. You may be working a new job that demands extra hours to make ends meet. These challenges will only make you stronger, preparing you for the next challenge. *This new, deeper self is a wonderful anchor for the struggles that lie ahead.*

Even in the midst of looking for her apartment, Jackie noticed that she felt stronger than she had in previous weeks. Something was energizing about moving forward in a positive direction. She began to enjoy being in her new place, decorating it exactly the way she liked, and pulling out her journal after her son went to bed to jot a few words about the day. She would use this gift of time to understand herself better. It was an exciting, albeit frightening, time. Listen to her thoughts on her recent separation and time of uncertainty.

"For many years I focused on pleasing others. I got my validation by being something to somebody. I thought my world would end when Daniel decided he no longer loved me. I had prepared myself for being a wife and mother, and my job was to keep the home stable. When he told me that he was no longer in love with me, it was like getting hit in the stomach with a sucker punch. For a while, I actually couldn't breathe. But I found some stability which allowed me to move forward with my life. I feel more independent and able to make decisions by myself, which I hadn't been before. I am learning that I cannot please everyone. All I can do is take care of myself and my son and listen to God's work in my life. I think that is a key to happiness."

Sixth, *be aware of bursts of creativity during difficult times and make use of them.* During times of crisis we often seek outlets for our creativity. These can be rich times of writing, composing music, painting, trying new things, or putting energy into familiar activities that bring you peace and pleasure.

Jackie had always felt close to her son, Timothy. This separation, however, caused her to appreciate him in new ways. They would face this adventure together, she decided. They would explore the world together, and she delighted in watching him grow during this tender time.

Jackie also cultivated her flowers and herbs, and she found her plants to be even more important to her at this time. She took special care in watering and nurturing them.

What creative talents do you possess? Are there any new ventures you want to take on?

Finally, *watch for the God winks*. Something quite amazing happens when we are on the lookout for those little reflections of God's grace in our lives. Why? Because they happen all the time, and we need to become more alert to them and enjoy them as anchors in our lives. Consider how you might feel if you realized that God was intimately familiar with you and your circumstances and was going to send you gifts—both large and small—throughout the day.

Squire Rushnell, author of *When God Winks*, reminds us that "A God wink is also a message of reassurance when you need it most: when you're at a crossroads in your life, and when instability is all around. It might be said, in fact, that coincidences are the best way for God to establish a perpetual presence in your life."[2]

Rushnell believes, as do I, that these God winks are purposeful. God is doing something bigger for us, and to us, than we can imagine or immediately understand. So keep your eyes open. Watch and listen. See what God is doing for you through those miraculous daily winks.

Jackie came home one evening and noticed that one of her Texas cactus plants that had never blossomed before had sprung to new life. She touched it gently and smiled. Was it a coincidence or a little love gift from God?

Learning to watch, look, and listen are powerful tools for gaining access to a fulfilling life. These tools are especially useful during times of crisis. Consider Rainer Maria Rilke's advice about learning to let life unfold at its own pace:

> Be patient toward all that is unsolved in your heart and try to love the questions themselves like locked rooms and like books that are written in a very foreign tongue. Do not seek the answers, which cannot be given you because you would not be able to live them. And the point is, to live everything. Live the questions now. Perhaps you will then gradually, without noticing it, live along some distant day into the answer.[3]

## Chrysalis

With anchors set, you are now able to be still and let the transformation take place. For this discussion, let's consider a new metaphor of the chrysalis, the cocoon where a caterpillar transforms into a butterfly. For us, this is where spiritual and emotional metamorphosis happens.

It is interesting to note that the word *crisis* comes from the Greek words *krisis* and *krino,* which mean "a separating." Here in the chrysalis, safe from the harshness of your personal winter, you are free to *wait for change.* During this time of separation from those things you once found comforting, you are able to reflect upon what you need now. You may be surprised at what you discover. You may be surprised at what emerges from the chrysalis. You will surely emerge a far different person than when you entered.

Darkness can be horrifying. Unable to see what is ahead and confused about what is behind, we are left to grope in the dark. You will probably feel terrified at times and want to break free, rushing back to the past or hurrying into the future. But go slowly. Remind yourself that you have

- places where you are safe and secure
- activities and hobbies that are nurturing to you
- people who are supportive
- a positive attitude and a renewed sense of purpose
- the knowledge that you will grow, becoming richer and deeper
- a rekindled sense of creativity
- God winks to guide you on your way

Rainier Maria Rilke, in *Letters to a Young Poet,* encourages us not to be afraid of this new aloneness. "And you should not let yourself be confused in your solitude by the fact that there is something in you that wants to break out of it. . . . People have (with the help of conventions) oriented all their solutions toward the easy and toward the easiest side of the easy; but it is clear that we must hold to what is difficult; . . . it is good to be solitary, for solitude is difficult; that something is difficult must be a reason the more for us to do it."[4]

### New Identity

If you have allowed yourself to enter the chrysalis and be changed by it, you are not the same person that entered this crisis. You are becoming a new and improved version of your former self. Consider some of the ways Jackie is different than she was before this crisis. Allow yourself to consider how you too can become new and improved.

Before this crisis *Jackie was timid and afraid of change.* While she is not finished with the entire process, she already feels much more capable of handling challenges. Whenever she began to feel frightened, she pictured herself handling the troubling situation with a sense of peace. Instead of slipping into her fear of loneliness, she made plans to have friends over to help her set up her apartment. She used a few extra dollars and focused her energies on making her apartment feel comfortable.

Before the separation *Jackie took everything very seriously.* People often told her to "lighten up." Now she is better able to see the humor in human troubles, including her own. She and some friends get together on a regular basis and are able to laugh at some of the humorous aspects of her situation. For example, she can laugh at how she has to pinch pennies and shop at Goodwill stores but delights in finding wonderful bargains in the process. While before she would never have wanted to buy secondhand things, she now proudly displays her "treasures."

Before the separation *Jackie would never ask for help.* Now she finds that she must reach out and call someone when she is feeling fragile. She is glad for the opportunity to call a friend and to ask for prayer. She has cultivated a strong list of friends who are available to her for talking, going out to a movie, or walking in the park when things look dreary. Her friends also made the move from her home to the apartment much easier.

Before the separation, *Jackie seldom reflected upon her contributions to marital problems.* Now she spends time every day writing in her prayer journal, often considering the various struggles she experienced in her marriage and her part in them. She is not afraid to slow down and reflect upon her day and the things she is learning. She is not afraid to feel the sadness that comes with leaving her home and husband.

Before the separation, *Jackie had lived an untested faith.* Now she has learned to lean on God for strength and wisdom. She has developed a deep faith through her practice of prayer and meditation. She has learned to talk to God and listen. She has created a devotional time every morning and evening where she prayerfully considers the things weighing on her heart.

Before the separation, *Jackie took her family, especially her parents, for granted.* While she attended various family functions, she was easily annoyed by the foibles of her family. She did not feel connected to them in a spiritual or emotional sense.

Through this crisis she has learned to trust her parents and siblings with her deepest hurts and fears, and it has brought them closer together. She now calls her mother several times a week to bounce ideas off her. She is surprised by her mother's wisdom. She feels safe in confiding in her mother and sister. They have become much closer to one another.

Before the separation, *Jackie was not aware of her emotions.* Now she enjoys journaling and bringing her pain before the Lord in prayer. She feels like she has more depth to her personality. While not ruled by emotion, Jackie now lets her emotions guide her into actions. Before the separation, *Jackie kept herself distant from the pain of others.* Having now experienced her own deep pain, she is able to honestly relate to others' struggles. She finds that she wants to be available to offer compassion and support to them.

Before the separation, *Jackie lived for the future* and was anxious about whether or not life would unfold the way she had hoped and planned. Now she finds herself enjoying the present, appreciating the gifts that each day has to offer. She no longer holds tightly to the script of how she expected life to be. Rather, she seeks out life's gifts and surprises.

You can see that this very troubling time for Jackie has resulted in many gifts for her. She has opened herself to new experiences and opportunities. Her friendships are deeper, her appreciation for life fuller, and her spiritual life richer. Does she know whether things with Daniel will work out? No. But she has learned to accept whatever happens.

**Stronger Than Before**

Perhaps you too have emerged from the chrysalis having learned to hold the tensions creatively and wait for change. Perhaps you have received a glimpse of the possibility that you can be stronger than before. Perhaps you have discovered parts of yourself that had been lost. This can be a wonderfully exciting time in your life, provided you think of it not simply as a crisis but as an opportunity.

Keep in mind that this is an opportunity not just for you but for your marriage as well. Hopefully your partner has used this time of separation for growth as well, though that may not be the case. Separations do not always have happy endings. While you may be stronger, your marriage may not be. What can be said about this?

First, *you can only be responsible for yourself.* You have grown stronger and developed a surer vision for your life. This may not be the case for your spouse. Your spouse may, for a variety of reasons, remain stuck in the muddle. Remember that it is their muddle and you can do little about it.

Second, *you have discovered that you are a better person because of this crisis.* You have let the sorrows of this experience settle, creating profound change. Rilke encourages us not to be a "waster of sorrows." He tells us, "The more still, more patient and more open we are when we are sad, so much the deeper and so much the more unswervingly does the new go into us, so much the better do we make it ours, so much the more will it be our destiny."[5]

Third, *you have realized that much of life unfolds in an unpredictable way.* You cannot control everything that happens. Hanging onto your own plans will only frustrate you. Hold onto life loosely, letting God do what he wants to do. You will be the better for it.

Many people move beyond lost love and separation, through the chrysalis of darkness into the light of either reconciliation or peace about the loss. They use their time apart wisely and come back together to form an alliance stronger than they had before. After time apart, they find their hearts warming toward each other. The old wounds seem to dissipate with time. The old challenges and road-blocks can be torn down with time and wise counsel.

You are different now than when you first separated. If you allow yourself enough time to "be with your sorrows" and reclaim lost parts of yourself, you will be equipped to make good choices about reconciliation.

## Summary

Love lost and separations are painful. However you resolve this crisis, you are in the process of change. You have experienced the darkness of separation, the loneliness known only by those who have been abandoned by a lover. This is not an easy time, but, thankfully, it can be a richly rewarding one. With newly found anchors, you can face any adversity that comes your way.

I hope that you have found in this book a companion for your journey. I know that grieving well and seeking ways to find the deeper meanings of this experience will be beneficial. Blessings to you as you continue your journey toward healing and wholeness.

# NOTES

## Chapter 1: Love Lost

1. Sue Monk Kidd, *When the Heart Waits* (San Francisco: HarperSanFrancisco, 1990).

2. John J. L. Mood, *Rilke on Love and Other Difficulties* (New York: Norton, 1975), 31.

3. M. Scott Peck, *The Road Less Traveled* (New York: Simon & Schuster, 1978).

## Chapter 2: The Mysterious Grief of Love Lost

1. Judith Viorst, *Necessary Losses* (New York: Simon & Schuster, 1986), 259.

2. Elisabeth Kübler-Ross, *On Death and Dying* (New York: Touchstone, 1997).

3. Thomas Whiteman and Randy Petersen, *Starting Over: A Step-by-Step Guide to Help You Rebuild Your Life After a Breakup* (Colorado Springs: Pinon Press, 2001).

4. Kari West and Noelle Quinn, *When He Leaves* (Colorado Springs: Chariot Victor, 1998), 66.

## Chapter 3: The Uncertainty of What's Next

1. Taken in part from the American Association for Marriage and Family Therapy, 1133 15th Street N.W., Suite 300, Washington DC.

2. Anthony Storr, *Solitude* (New York: Ballantine, 1988), 22.

3. Ibid., 34.

## Chapter 4: Vulnerability

1. Michael Downey, "Brief Gold," *Weavings,* July/August 1993, 19.

2. Dorothy Briggs, *Celebrate Yourself* (New York: Doubleday, 1977), 127.

3. Sidney Simon, "Caring, Feeling, Touching," from a manual titled *Surviving Your Loss, Rebuilding Your Life,* 90.

4. Henri Nouwen, *The Inner Voice of Love* (New York: Doubleday, 1996), 9.

## Chapter 5: The Ride

1. Jack Williamson and Mary Ann Salerno, *Divorce: Six Ways to Get through the Bad Times* (New York: Bridge Builder Media, 2001), 26.

2. Ibid., 35.

3. Quoted in William Barclay, *The Gospel of Luke* (Laurinburg, NC: Saint Andrews Press, 1953).

4. Micki McWade, *Getting Up, Getting Over, Getting On* (Beverly Hills, CA: Champion Press, 1999), 71.

5. John Gottman, *The Seven Principles for Making Marriage Work* (New York: Random House, 1999), 27–33.

## Chapter 6: Friendship in Times of Need

1. Whiteman and Petersen, *Starting Over,* 169.

2. Melba Colgrove, Harold Bloomfield, and Peter McWilliams, *How to Survive the Loss of a Love* (Los Angeles: Bantam, 1976), 60.

## Chapter 7: Family Matters

1. Ellen Sue Stern, *Divorce Is Not the End of the World* (Berkeley: Tricycle Press, 1997), 9.

2. Rita and John Sommers-Flannigan and Chelsea Elander, *Don't Divorce Us* (Alexandria, VA: American Counseling Association, 2000), 22.

3. Ibid., 84.

4. Ibid., 15.

## Chapter 8: Searching for Silver

1. Peck, *The Road Less Traveled*, 15.

2. John DeMartini, *Count Your Blessings* (London, England: HarperCollins, 1997), 11–16.

3. Joseph Stowell, *Through the Fire* (Wheaton: Victor, 1985), 30.

4. Alexandra Stoddard, *The Art of the Possible* (New York: William Morrow, 1995), 243.

5. Terry Hershey, *Beginning Again: Life After a Relationship Ends* (Nashville: Thomas Nelson, 1986), 41.

6. Stoddard, *The Art of the Possible*, 244.

## Chapter 9: Crucible for Change

1. William Bridges, *The Way of Transition* (Cambridge: Perseus, 2001), 62–63.

2. M. Robert Muholland, "Life in the Desert," *Weavings*, May/June 2001, 22.

3. Kidd, *When the Heart Waits*, 43.

## Chapter 10: Considering Reconciliation

1. Sidney and Suzanne Simon, *Forgiveness: How to Make Peace with Your Past and Get On with Your Life* (New York: Warner Books, 1991), 138.

2. Tian Dayton, *The Magic of Forgiveness* (Deerfield Beach, Fla.: Health Communications, 2003).

3. Ibid., 61.

4. Ibid., 64.

5. Susan Heitler, *The Power of Two* (Oakland: New Harbinger, 1997), 184–186.

6. Wayne Dyer, *There is a Spiritual Solution to Every Problem* (New York: HarperCollins, 2003), 27.

7. Heitler, *The Power of Two,* 186.

8. Dyer, *There is a Spiritual Solution to Every Problem,* 133.

## Chapter 11: Embracing Community, Encouraging Church

1. Mitch Albom, *Tuesdays with Morrie* (New York: Doubleday, 1997), 134.

2. Stoddard, *The Art of the Possible,* 170.

3. Henry Cloud and John Townsend, *Boundaries* (Grand Rapids: Zondervan, 1999), 17.

4. Paul Escamilla, "Something Bigger Than All of Us," *Weavings,* July/August 1995, 27.

5. John Bradshaw, *Healing the Shame That Binds* (Deerfield Beach, Fla.: Health Communications, 1988), 18–19.

6. Ron and Vicki Burks, *Damaged Disciples* (Grand Rapids: Zondervan, 1992).

7. David Seamands, *Healing for Damaged Emotions* (Grand Rapids: Zondervan, 1985), 79–83.

8. Brennan Manning, *The Ragamuffin Gospel* (Sisters, Ore.: Multnomah, 2000), 181.

## Chapter 12: New Moorings

1. Alexandra Stoddard, *Gracious Living in a New World* (New York: William Morrow and Company, 1996), 166.

2. Squire Rushnell, *When God Winks* (Hillsboro, Ore.: Beyond Words Publishing, 2001), 4.

3. Rainer Maria Rilke, *Letters to a Young Poet* (New York: Norton, 1934), 35

4. Ibid., 53.

5. Ibid., 79.

**Dr. David B. Hawkins** regularly counsels hurting couples as a licensed clinical psychologist and social worker with a private practice in Longview, Washington. He has hosted radio and television broadcasts on abuse and domestic violence. He is the author of several books, including most recently *Does Your Man Have the Blues?*